BTEC
BUSINESS
ASSESSMENT GUIDE

Unit 1 ENTERPRISE IN THE
BUSINESS WORLD

Unit 2 FINANCE FOR BUSINESS

CAROLE TROTTER
IAN GUNN

HODDER
EDUCATION
AN HACHETTE UK COMPANY

The sample learner answers provided in this assessment guide are intended to give guidance on how a learner might approach generating evidence for each assessment criterion. Answers do not necessarily include all of the evidence required to meet each assessment criterion. Assessor comments intend to highlight how sample answers might be improved to help learners meet the requirements of the grading criterion but are provided as a guide only. Sample answers and assessor guidance have not been verified by Edexcel and any information provided in this guide should not replace your own internal verification process.

Any work submitted as evidence for assessment for this unit must be the learner's own. Submitting as evidence, in whole or in part, any material taken from this guide will be regarded as plagiarism. Hodder Education accepts no responsibility for learners plagiarising work from this guide that does or does not meet the assessment criteria.

The sample assignment briefs are provided as a guide to how you might assess the evidence required for all or part of the internal assessment of this Unit. They have not been verified or endorsed by Edexcel and should be internally verified through your own Lead Internal Verifier as with any other assignment briefs, and/or checked through the BTEC assignment checking service.

Every effort has been made to trace the copyright holders of material reproduced here. The authors and publishers would like to thank the following for permission to reproduce copyright illustrations.

Figure 1.1 © bloomua – Fotolia; Figure 1.2 © djma – Fotolia; Figure 1.3 © pizuttipics – Fotolia; Figure 1.4 © zentilia – Fotolia; Figure 1.5 © Dyson; Figure 1.6 © picsfive – Fotolia; Figure 1.7 © Minerva Studio – Fotolia; Figure 1.8 © 1997 Steve Mason/Photodisc/Getty Images; Figure 1.9 © James Cook/Rex Features; Figure 1.10 © David Bagnall/Rex Features; Figure 1.12 © CandyBox Images – Fotolia; Figure 2.2 © Monkey Business – Fotolia; Figure 2.3 © djtaylor – Fotolia.

Orders: please contact Bookpoint Ltd, 130 Milton Park, Abingdon, Oxon OX14 4SB. Telephone: (44) 01235 827720. Fax: (44) 01235 400454. Lines are open from 9am to 5pm, Monday to Saturday, with a 24-hour message answering service. You can also order through our website www.hoddereducation.co.uk

If you have any comments to make about this, or any of our other titles, please send them to educationenquiries@hodder.co.uk

British Library Cataloguing in Publication Data

A catalogue record for this title is available from the British Library

ISBN: 978 1444 18677 2

This edition published 2013

Impression number   10 9 8 7 6 5 4 3 2 1

Year   2016, 2015, 2014, 2013

Copyright © 2013 Carole Trotter and Ian Gunn

Cover photo © Paulus Nugroho R – Fotolia

Typeset by Integra Software Services Pvt. Ltd, Pondicherry, India

Printed in Dubai for Hodder Education, an Hachette UK Company, 338 Euston Road, London NW1 3BH

Contents

For attention of the learner

You are not allowed to copy any information from this book and use it as your own evidence. That would count as plagiarism, which is taken very seriously and may result in disqualification. If you are in any doubt at all please speak to your teacher.

Command words

There are numerous terms or command verbs that will be used in the specification. Most of them are very straightforward as follows:

Outline	Write a clear description but not a detailed one.
Describe	Give a clear description that includes all the relevant features; think of it as 'painting a picture with words'.
Explain	Set out in detail the meaning of something, with reasons. More difficult than describe or list, so it can help to give an example to show what you mean. Start by introducing the topic, then give the 'how' or 'why'.
Compare	Identify the main factors that apply in two or more situations and explain the similarities and differences or advantages and disadvantages.
Assess	Give careful consideration to all the factors or events that apply and identify which are the most important or relevant.
Justify	Give reasons or evidence to support your opinion or view, to show how you arrived at these conclusions.

UNIT 1
Enterprise in the business world

Enterprise in the Business World is an internally assessed core unit with three learning aims. It focuses on the importance of knowing and understanding the current business environment and current trends when planning a new business venture. You need to understand:

- the importance of planning
- the importance of investigating the market
- how outside influences can affect a business venture.

This unit also provides an opportunity to plan and present your own business start-up plan.

This part of the book includes:

- Guidance on each learning aim – all the topics in the learning aims should be studied, and the book includes useful suggestions for each. Examples are included, but these could be replaced by local examples from your area.
- Evidence generated by a learner for each assessment criterion, with feedback from an assessor. The assessor has highlighted where the evidence is sufficient to satisfy the grading criterion, and provided developmental feedback when additional work is required. This material provides support for assessment.
- Examples of assignment briefs, with clear guidance on the evidence you will need to generate and submit for each grading criterion, and the format in which the evidence should be submitted.

Answers to the knowledge recap questions provided in the learning aim summaries can be found at the back of the book.

Learning aim A
Know how trends and the current business environment may impact on a business

Assessment criteria

2A.P1 Outline how the business environment can impact on a start-up business.

2A.P2 Explain how current trends will impact on a start-up business.

2A.M1 Explain how changes in the current business environment are likely to impact on a start-up business.

2A.M2 Compare how two trends have impacted on a start-up business.

2A.D1 Assess the current risks, opportunities and trends in the business environment for a start-up business.

Learning aim A provides an opportunity to get a better understanding of the factors and trends that have an impact on any new businesses.

Finding information

Doing your own research is important. A lot of the information about how trends and the current business environment may have an impact on a business will come from researching the current business environment and researching topics such as the cost of borrowing money or getting a mortgage, changes to taxation, trends, local factors and the support for businesses.

It is important to use more than one source of research and identify the source of your information in your assignment work. Where possible both **primary** and **secondary** sources should be used.

Primary sources

Studied

These are original sources from which you gather your own information. Typically, these will include letters to businesses (or similar) for information, questionnaires to collect opinions, and surveys of local competition. Present the results from a questionnaire in an appropriate way to support your findings as this will help validate any judgements you make. Line graphs for continuous data, bar charts for discrete data and pie charts for percentages are particularly good ways to present the information. Include all data in an appendix.

Secondary sources

Essentially these are other people's primary sources. Secondary sources could include the internet, magazines, TV and company background data. Always try to check the data against another source to ensure its validity and to make sure it is up to date.

Online sources

There are several websites that provide information on national statistics that would be beneficial when researching trends and the current business environment (see, for example, www.statistics.gov.uk). You should always be aware that on some websites some of the information or data may be historical and not current. It is always worth checking data from two or more sources to ensure it is reliable.

The internet is a good research tool with lots of information and facts on current events. Some websites do provide information on the impact that some of these factors are having on the business environment but you need to be aware that, on occasion, these may be biased and just the views or conclusions of one person.

Figure 1.1 Many readers access broadsheet newspapers online

Newspaper sources

All broadsheet newspapers provide current information and updates on the business environment. The broadsheets provide up-to-date information on any changes to interest rates, taxation and the exchange rate, and will usually summarise the impact these will have on the business world. They can be accessed online as well as in traditional paper format.

Local newspapers will provide information on the impact that the current business environment is having on the local area; this is important since, for learning aims B and C, you will be focusing on setting up a business venture in the local area.

Magazines

Professional and trade journals provide information and articles on the impact that current factors and trends have had on different markets.

Local advice

Anyone thinking about setting up a new business venture will need support and advice. There is a lot of support and guidance available from business networking organisations for new business ventures. You will find a list of local business-networking organisations and a summary of the support they offer on the internet. Sites such as **www.salesexchange.co.uk/business-to-business-networking/ business-to-business-networking-sites** are a useful source of information.

Factors to consider in the current business environment

When planning to set up a new business there are a number of factors you will need to consider. The factors are divided into two main sections: national factors and local factors. You will need to know and understand that national and local factors will have an impact on any business, new or existing. The change in any factor is often outside the control of the management of a business but might have an impact on any element of their business and the decisions they make for the future. You will need to know what is happening in the current business environment.

National factors

Political issues and government support

It is important to research current political issues that might affect the business environment, as well as current government support and the guidance that is available for existing businesses, as well as the support that is available for new businesses.

The economy

It is important to understand which factors can impact on the business environment. Some of the important ones are:

- Cost of borrowing/loans – the impact of any increase or fall in interest rates; a fall in interest rates will mean that consumers may be willing to borrow and spend more, which is good news for businesses.
- Taxation – the increase or fall in corporation tax and VAT will affect the price the consumer pays for the goods or service.
- Inflation – inflation is the rise and fall in the price customers pay for goods or services. A rise in inflation will mean that consumers will get less for their money.
- Employment – an increase in the number of unemployed people will reduce the amount of money consumers will have to spend and their confidence in spending.
- Exchange rates – if the pound is strong against other currencies a business will get more for their money when buying supplies from another country.

Local factors

It is important to understand how local factors can have an impact on the business environment:

- Location – it is important to find the correct location for a business; the business will need to consider the appropriate location for access and transportation and to attract customers.
- Resources – a business will need to know where to obtain essential equipment and materials, and also be able to employ staff with the correct skills and knowledge.
- Competitors – a business will need to know who the competitors are and what they do.
- Customers – a business will need to identify their target market, such as teenagers, mothers, the elderly.

You will need to understand the impact of both national and local factors on your own business idea and your target consumer groups. It would be beneficial to focus on your business idea when researching national and local factors.

Figure 1.2 Some products are marketed at particular groups, such as teenagers

Trends affecting business

Changes in trends will have an impact on a business and the demand for products and services. Trends can be social, technological, environmental and ethical. You will need to investigate how changes in each of these types of trend will have an impact on business ventures.

Social trends

Studied ☐

Social trends focus on several elements including population changes, the make-up of households and family units, changes in education and the labour market.

Any change in the population statistics will have an impact on the demand for some goods and services. For example, people are living longer and so there will be an increase in the demand for care and support facilities, medicines and some leisure pursuits. A fall in the number of births will see a decline in the purchase of products for babies, such as nursery furniture, nappies and baby clothes.

There are changes in households and the family unit, with fewer marriages and children living part of the week with one parent and the rest of the week with the other. A decline in marriages will see a fall in the demand for wedding dresses and accessories. Smaller family units will see a decrease in demand for some household products.

A change in education trends might see more students achieving improved outcomes in their exams and deciding to remain in education. An increase in unemployment figures might see people looking at retraining and maybe even returning to full- or part-time education. An increase in the number of people in education will bring an increase in demand for stationery, books and computers.

The labour market is constantly changing, with more women returning to full-time employment and sometimes even being the main wage earner. For businesses this will cause an increase in demand for childcare and formal working clothes. More and more companies are offering flexible working hours, which could cause an increase in the demand for leisure pursuits but perhaps also a fall in demand for childcare facilities.

With people having to relocate or commute to large towns or cites to use their skills there will be an increase in the demand for transport, petrol and travel facilities.

Technology trends

Changes in technology will have an impact on most businesses. A business can set up online and reach a wider market, 24 hours a day. The internet provides an opportunity for a business to monitor competitive activity and to investigate where and how to get support. A business will be able to design websites that provide detailed information on their products and services.

Developments in telephony – such as the ability to shop, bank and pay via mobile phones; access offers via email on mobile phones and transfer cash via apps on mobile phones – will provide the opportunity for a business to keep in constant contact with both customers and suppliers.

Figure 1.3 Mobile phone technology has created new opportunities for businesses

Environmental trends

Renewable energy is becoming increasingly important as we become more aware of the effects of climate change. There have been significant developments in using wind and solar power to supply our energy needs.

Consumers are more aware of environmental issues and will look for products that are energy efficient and recyclable. An example of this is the increase in the demand for energy-efficient light bulbs and a fall in the sale of conventional light bulbs. Customers will choose a product that is simply packaged and cheaper over the same product in decorative packaging, usually with a higher price tag.

Figure 1.4

Learning aim A: Know how trends and the current business environment may impact on a business

Ethical trends

Studied ☐

Customers are more aware of their carbon footprint (the level of greenhouse gases they create, which has an effect on climate change) and this might have an impact on the products they buy.

Customers will be reluctant to buy products that are linked to child labour but might buy products to support developing countries, such as fair-trade products. Customers may be reluctant to purchase products that have been tested on animals and so demand for these products will fall.

Consumers may want to support their local small businesses so will purchase products such as cakes or jam that have been made locally rather than purchasing the same product from a supermarket.

Size of business and type

Businesses come in different sizes and types. The amount of support, loans, grants and government advice each needs is determined by the number of staff employed by the business, the business turnover and the profit margin. There is a lot of information available about financial support and advice and guidance for new businesses, and daily updates are available in the broadsheet newspapers, the radio and television media, and on the internet.

Micro business

Studied ☐

A micro business is often a small sole trader and occasionally a partnership that has up to nine staff. A micro business is often one that has been developed from a hobby or interest. There is a lot of advice and guidance on how to set up a business available on the internet and from local organisations.

Small and medium enterprises

Studied ☐

Small and medium enterprises (SMEs) are businesses that employ fewer than 250 staff. A small business will employ fewer than 50 people; a medium business employs between 50 and 249 people. A lot of new businesses are SMEs, which are seen to be important to the growth of the UK economy. Over the past few years there has been an increase in the number of SMEs that have been started by minority ethnic groups and women.

Large business

Studied ☐

A large business is a business with more than 250 staff and is usually managed by shareholders. A large business will be divided into functional departments and may have several branches in different locations nationally and maybe even globally.

Start-ups

Studied ☐

A start-up business is a new business venture and time and money will need to have been spent to investigate if the business is viable. The start-up business will begin with someone having an idea for a business. The resources and financial requirements for a start-up business will depend on the product or service offered and the size of the business.

Existing business

Studied ☐

An existing business is a business that is already up, running and trading. The business will already have a name, a known product, premises, resources and employees and, most importantly, a reputation.

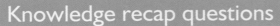
1. All businesses need to have information about competitors, finance and location. Identify three sources of useful information.

2. Information is easily available online. State two reasons why you need to be careful when using this information.

3. Any new business is affected by external factors and it has to work with them and adapt to them. These factors can be national, i.e. they affect **any** business, or local, i.e. they **only** affect that business.

   a. List three national factors that affect a business.

   b. List three local factors that affect a business.

4. The four main categories of trends affecting a business are shown in the table below (social, ethical, technological and environmental). Put the trends listed below into the correct category in the table.

   Carbon footprint, flexitime, online shopping, testing on animals, recyclable materials, use of solar panels, working from home, mobile barcode scanning

Social	Ethical	Technological	Environmental

5. Businesses are put into categories depending on how many people they employ. This can affect how much support they are entitled to. How many staff does each of the following business types employ?

   a. Micro

   b. Small

   c. Medium

   d. Large

6. Describe some advantages of a going into an existing business rather than starting up your own.

7. Describe some disadvantages of going into an existing business rather than starting up on your own.

Assessment guidance for learning aim A

2A.P1 **Outline how the business environment can impact on a start-up business**

✏️ Learner answer

There are several factors that could have an impact on a start-up business. The factors are: inflation, costs of getting a loan, currency, start-up loans, interest rates, changes to laws, recession, location, customers and the competitors.

Assessor report: The learner has only listed the factors and will now need to **outline** how these factors could have an impact on a start-up business. This means that they need to write a clear (but not necessarily detailed) description of how the factors can impact on a start-up business.

I will explain how factors will have an impact on a start-up business.

Factor	How it affects a business
Increase in inflation	An increase in inflation will mean an increase in the price of goods, so the business will have to pay more for what they want to buy, such as materials.
Cost of a loan	If you need to borrow money and interest rates go up you will need to pay more for the loan.
Currency	
Start-up loans	You may need to have a lot of money to put into the business before you can get a loan; the government has encouraged banks to support new businesses but it may still be difficult to get any type of loan.
Laws	
Recession	In a recession people will not have money to spend and will not spend money on goods that are not necessary.
Location	

(Continued)

| Customers | You will need to know what customers want and then produce goods that customers want to buy; you will need to sell your product but will want to make some profit. |
| Competitors | You will need to offer different products to other local shops in the area; you will need to look at their stock and prices so that you can compete with them. |

Assessor report: The learner has used a range of local and national factors and **outlined** how they could have an impact on a start-up business. While the learner has listed a good range of factors, three of them have not been outlined, but just named.

Assessor report – overall

Is the evidence sufficient to satisfy the grading criterion?

The first part of the learner's evidence sets the scene and they have listed some of the factors in the business environment that could have an impact on a start-up business. The learner has gone on to develop a table, with column one listing the factors and column two outlining how each factor could have an impact on a start-up business.

What could be improved?

The learner has not provided sufficient evidence for the P1 grading criterion as they need to outline how the other three factors noted (currency, laws and location) can impact on a start-up business. The learner could have been encouraged to focus on the factors that would have most impact on their ideas for a start-up business.

2A.P2 Explain how current trends will impact on a start-up business

✍ Learner answer

There are several trends that could have an impact on a start-up business. The trends include social trends, such as an increase in children staying in education longer, people living longer, smaller families, people moving from area to area to find work, more women in full-time work, flexible working, and longer working hours. Other trends are developments in technology, looking after and caring for the environment, and animal welfare and supporting developing countries, such as buying fair-trade products.

Assessor report: The learner has listed a wide range of current trends but, to satisfy the grading criterion, will now need to explain how these trends will impact on a start-up business. This means they need to set out in detail how the current trends will impact on a start-up business. It can help to give an example to show what you mean. Start by introducing the topic and then give the 'how'.

Technology has made it easy for a business to keep in contact with customers and suppliers by the use of email and the internet. The internet allows a business to sell for longer hours and to sell goods in lots of different countries and to people who do not leave their homes or who work long hours. A start-up business will be able to advertise their goods on a website, which could be seen by lots of customers.

Assessor report: The learner has given a good explanation of how advancements in technology will have an impact on a start-up business. They will now need to focus on other trends.

A business would need to think about products that customers need and the age of the customers they want to sell goods to. People are living longer and people are retiring early, which means they will have more time for hobbies and more time to shop for bargains, but may not have a lot of money to spend. People who work long hours have no time to spare so they may want to buy all their products in one place, such as a supermarket, so small businesses will have to sell goods that are different to those sold in a supermarket. People are now more aware about environmental issues and will look for goods such as energy-saving light bulbs, which last longer and do not use as much electricity. Customers may also look for items that are cheaper because there is no extra packaging, such as see-through wrapping rather than boxes.

Assessor report: The learner has **explained** how a range of current trends may affect a start-up business. The learner could have focused a little more on the different aspects of social trends such as people staying in education longer, high unemployment rates for teenagers and young people, fewer marriages but an increase in people living together or sharing rents and mortgages. The learner has not made a reference to ethical trends, however.

Assessor report – overall

Is the evidence sufficient to satisfy the grading criterion?

In the first section the learner has just listed the current trends that could have an impact on a start-up business. The learner has then gone on to explain how technology, population changes, knowledge of environmental issues and support for developing countries could have an impact on a start-up business. The learner has, on a few occasions, provided examples to support their statements. The learner has not submitted sufficient evidence to satisfy the P2 grading criterion.

What could be improved?

The learner should be encouraged to focus on the trends that will have an impact on their ideas for a start-up business. Ethical issues are always current and will affect any new business – these should have been included. It would also have been useful to include some figures, such as age demographics, to support their findings. This would make it easier to validate the criterion.

(2A.M1) Explain how changes in the current business environment are likely to impact on a start-up business

✍ Learner answer

The interest rates have been low for some time, which means that the interest on any bank loan is low and people may borrow more money or buy more on credit. The current interest rate is 0.50 per cent, and on the www.thisismoney.co.uk website it says that interest rates will fall to 0.25 per cent, which may mean that people will borrow more.

The government is encouraging banks to lend money to small businesses but the newspapers are still saying that the loans are not available, so it may be difficult for a new business to obtain a loan. Interest rates are low, which means customers will be prepared to buy large items on credit because they do not have to pay high interest on the money they have borrowed. When interest rates are low customers will buy more luxury products but any rise will mean that customers will buy essential items and not luxuries. A fall in interest rates will make people borrow more but any increase will mean customers will not buy on credit, so the demand for products may fall.

Low interest rates will not be good for a business that has made any profit and wants to save, because they would only get a small amount of interest on their savings.

Assessor report: The learner has made a very good start in **explaining** the impact of changes to interest rates. This means that they have set out in detail, with reasons, how the changes are likely to impact on a start-up business. They will now need to explain how other factors will have an impact on a start-up business. The learner has referenced a website used for information on current interest rates. The learner has clearly highlighted that a newspaper was a source of information, demonstrating that the internet is *not* the only source.

The newspapers and television are highlighting that there is no improvement and that the UK is still in recession. Talk about the recession will mean that customers are not spending, so it may be difficult to build up my new business. Lots of small shops and well-known shops have closed, which means that people are unemployed and will not have money to spend on non-essential items such as my bracelets and charms, but customers may still want a treat and my charms are cheap to buy. A fall in sales may mean that a business would not be able to pay their bills and the interest payments for any loans, so the first thing they will do is get rid of employees.

Assessor report: The learner has briefly **explained** how the recession may have an impact on a start-up business and has also highlighted the impact on consumer spending. The learner has correctly noted that a fall in sales will lead to unemployment but not how that, in turn, would affect a start-up business.

The government is trying to support start-up businesses by changing taxes such as corporation tax. A rise in corporation tax will mean that a business will keep more of its profits, which it can use to help the business grow.

Value-added tax is added to the price of many products and this adds to the cost of the product for the customer. I would need to know if my bracelets and charms were exempt from VAT.

The government is trying to help customers and has added more items into the zero-rated section.

The government has also introduced several different business start-up grants and support schemes for new businesses. There is lots of information on the internet about grants for new business, such as www.startups.co.uk/grants-for-starting-a-business, where I got my information. There are repayable grants and soft loans but the website says it is difficult to get the money. A new business may need help in finding out about loans and grants, and how to fill in the paperwork. Some grants are just available in some areas and others are for small and medium enterprises with staff numbers below 250. There are other schemes available just for small businesses with staff numbers below 150.

Assessor report: The third section of the learner's work highlights how the government is supporting start-up businesses, but the learner's evidence for this grading criterion is focused entirely on national factors. The learner included some factual errors and these will need correcting. The learner has incorrectly stated that a rise in corporation tax will mean more profits for the business and that a small business will have fewer than 150 staff.

Assessor report – overall

Is the evidence sufficient to satisfy the grading criterion?

In the first section the learner has produced a good explanation on how changes in interest rates will affect a business. The learner has developed their evidence for this grading criterion by explaining the impact of the recession and changes to corporation tax on a business. The learner has highlighted that there is government support available for start-up businesses. With amendments to the factual information, the learner would have submitted work sufficient for the M1 grading criterion.

What could be improved?

The learner has focused on national factors and should be encouraged to include the impact of local factors on a start-up business, such as enterprise grants, unemployment projects and local council initiatives.

(2A.M2) Compare how two trends have impacted on a start-up business

✎ Learner answer

The developments in technology will provide more opportunities for new businesses. A business will have access to internet and email but also to improvements in telephony. The developments in technology such as online shopping and mobile phone apps will benefit people who are working longer hours and especially the increase in the number of working mums. Changes in people's lifestyles will make them want to find easy ways to shop. Access to online shopping will help elderly customers who cannot get to local towns.

Assessor report: The learner has identified that the two trends they will compare are technology and social trends. The learner will now need to compare how these trends have impacted on a start-up business. This means they will need to explain the similarities and differences between how the two trends have impacted on a start-up business. It would be beneficial for them to link the trends to a business they know well.

The developments in technology have made it easier for a start-up business to advertise to a wide range of different customers. The design of a website will provide the opportunity for a business to show their products and to clearly explain what they can do. The online shop is open 24 hours a day, seven days a week — much longer than a town centre or even a 24/7 supermarket, which close late on Saturday evenings and open for a few hours on Sunday. Argos sells charms and does advertise online, so customers could buy 24/7.

Developments in mobile telephones mean that people can talk on the move, so customers can contact shops to order products or staff can discuss problems without coming into the shop or office. A small start-up business could use a voicemail service for when they are out, which means they will not lose customers.

Assessor report: The learner has explained some important impacts of the developments in technology but is still not providing any comparison. The learner will need to compare the similarities and the differences of technology and social trends. This is currently insufficient to gain the M2 grading criterion.

People today have very different lifestyles and more women are working full time, which provides little spare time for looking around for special offers or bargains. Some people need to travel to large towns or city centres to find a job that uses the skills they have worked hard to get and, again, will have no spare time to look around for products or bargains. Other people may choose to work flexible hours but this may be to allow them to collect children from school or to look after elderly parents. The people who choose flexible working hours may still not have time to shop around for products. The lack of free time will mean that customers will look for a quick and easy way to shop for products and this may be online shopping.

Technology developments provide the opportunity for a start-up business to trade online 24/7. The start-up business can provide the opportunity for the customers to buy their products from the comfort of their homes or during a lunch break at work. The change in customers' working and social lifestyles mean that they do not have the time to walk around shopping malls and now have the advantage of purchasing products from the start-up business from their homes or their workplace 24/7. So, the developments in technology, which provides the start-up business with the opportunity to sell 24/7, is also an advantage for customers whose lifestyles have changed due to longer working days.

More people are living longer and elderly people may not be able to get out to do their shopping, so it is an advantage for them to have access to the things they need to buy online. A start-up business will be able to use technology developments to target customers, such as the elderly, who cannot get to the shops. This will be an advantage for a start-up business that uses technology developments and for their elderly customers.

People today work long hours and sometimes their working day is very long because they do not work in the area where they live. They can keep in contact with the start-up business because more people today have access to email and mobile phones. Developments in technology also mean that the start-up business will be able to keep in regular contact with its customers when they are not at home. So, the advantage for both the start-up business and changes in customers' lifestyles mean that they can still communicate with each other.

Assessor report: The learner has compared advantages for the changes in some social trends with technology developments but has made no reference to the disadvantages.

Assessor report – overall

Is the evidence sufficient to satisfy the grading criterion?

The learner has explained the advantages of developments in technology with the advantages for customers whose lifestyles have changed. The learner will need to develop their evidence to include a comparison of the disadvantages.

For example, a disadvantage for a start-up business in advertising their products online is that customers will not be able to view the products before they buy. This is also a disadvantage for busy customers who want to see clearly what they are spending their money on and whose busy lifestyles do not provide the time to return the products and request replacements.

What additional evidence, if any, is required?

To achieve M2 the learner will need to compare the disadvantages of developments in technology and changes in social trends. It may be useful or beneficial for the learners to present the points for comparison in a table with clearly defined sections to address.

Assess the current risks, opportunities and trends in the business environment for a start-up business

The learner is asked to assess the current risks, opportunities and trends. This means they need to give careful consideration to all of these factors and identify which are the most important or relevant.

✍ Learner answer

The following are factors and trends that will have an impact on any new business. I have listed the risks and opportunities for these factors and trends.

Factor or trend	Risk	Opportunity
Inflation	This could increase, which would mean that the price of materials would be more.	
Cost of a loan	A rise would mean you would pay more for a loan or mortgage; it would costs more to buy things on credit.	The interest rate is low so you would pay less interest on a mortgage; the interest rate could go lower so it would cost less for a mortgage or loan.
Currency	The countries that have the euro may change to other currencies.	Problems with the euro, mean the rate is good for the British.
Recession	If the recession goes on it will mean more people are unemployed and lots of businesses will close.	Things will get better when the recession is over.
Location	Some locations are poor but the rent will be cheap.	The location could be good for getting customers.
Customers	Customers shop around for goods that are cheap and different.	Customers will come again if they like the goods.
Competitors	More competitors move into the area.	Competitors go away or sells different goods.
Suppliers		Look for cheaper suppliers.
Changes in population	People retire from jobs and have little money to spend; there are lots of unemployed people with no money.	More elderly people.

Technology	This costs a lot of money if it breaks down and costs money to repair.	Can get to more people.
Environment		Cheaper to use less packaging.
Ethical	Many fair-trade products cost more; you have to think about what you say in adverts.	People will want to support local shops.

Assessor report: The learner has produced a good list of the factors and trends, but has currently only **described** the risks and opportunities for each factor and trend, and not made any clear **assessment**. They need to complete all sections of the table, not just those where there may appear to be an obvious answer. To assess any factor, the learner will need to look at both risks and opportunities.

The current risk to any new business would be an increase in interest rates, which means that they would have to pay more for loans, mortgages or for any items they purchase on credit. But the *Telegraph* newspaper says that the Bank of England will not increase the rate until 2013 or maybe 2014. The BBC News website says that interest rates were at 5 per cent in 2008 but have been at 0.5 per cent since March 2009, which is the lowest they have been and would be good news for any new business. The low interest rates mean people could have the opportunity to borrow money for a mortgage, but they may worry that there may be an increase and they would not be able to afford to keep the shop, so the move may not be a wise one.

Lots of companies advertise loans but the interest rates are not very good and some companies charge more money for paperwork. The interest rate for a loan on the Norton Finance website is 9.9 per cent or 17.9 per cent, but they also help people who have debt problems so you could get more and more into debt. It may be easy to get a loan to buy stock but if you cannot pay the money back you will get more into debt.

Getting the finances right is extremely important for a start-up business so this factor is really important.

Assessor report: The learner has provided a detailed description on the impact of changes in the interest rates and has **assessed** the impact of changes in interest rates, for example noting that although low rates are helpful now a change may prove that taking on a mortgage was not a good idea. They will now need to make reference to other factors and trends and then identify which are the most important and why.

People are living longer but a lot of elderly people only have a pension so will only buy what they need and will not buy luxury goods. A business could decide that it would be an opportunity to make a product for the elderly that will help them to keep active and busy.

Lots of people are working longer hours or have to travel a long way to work and back, so they will not want to spend a long time shopping. Lots of women are working full time as well as having a busy family life, so they will also not have a lot of time to shop.

Lots of people have lost their jobs or never had a job, so they will not have a lot of money to spend. People will buy what they need and will not spend money on luxury goods.

Assessor report: The learner is describing how social trends will have an impact on consumers' shopping habits but has not concluded by assessing which are the most important or relevant factors. The learner could be encouraged to include relevant data and the source to support their comments.

Assessor report – overall

Is the evidence sufficient to satisfy the grading criterion?

The learner has produced a good table that identifies several factors and trends. The learner has gone on to describe, in some detail, the impact of changes in the interest rates and has started to describe how the changes in social trends have an impact on consumers' buying habits. The learner has set the scene but has not yet concluded by assessing which are the most important factors, although interest rates have been covered well. The learner will need to do the same for the other factors and trends they mention in order to satisfy the requirements of the D1 grading criterion.

What additional evidence, if any, is required?

To achieve the D1 grading criterion the learner will need to include a little more information on local factors and trends. The learner should include relevant data or research to support their comments and reference the source. The learner will then need to conclude by assessing which are the most important factors or trends.

Learning aim B
Plan an idea for a new business

Assessment criteria

2B.P3 Describe, using relevant examples, the features of successful businesses.

2B.P4 Prepare a realistic initial plan for a business idea suitable for the local area.

2B.M3 Compare the features, strengths and weaknesses of two successful businesses.

2B.M4 Explain how the initial plan for a business idea has the potential to respond to market needs.

2B.D2 Justify how the initial plan for a business idea has potential for success in relation to existing local businesses.

Learning aim B provides the opportunity to plan a new business idea. You will need to investigate businesses that you feel are successful and then introduce your own idea for a start-up business.

How business ideas can be successful

There are a range of factors that make a business successful. You will need to investigate a range of successful businesses and, where possible, focus on investigating successful local entrepreneurs.

Innovative solutions

Businesses are often successful if they find an innovative solution for something. Dyson finding a solution to improving the vacuum cleaner is an example of an innovative solution that has been successful. James Dyson wanted to design a vacuum cleaner that worked more efficiently than conventional cleaners, which often got clogged up. He solved it by designing a system to filter and remove dust from the airflow, which meant there could be no clogging up or loss of suction.

Studied ☐

Figure 1.5 A Dyson design

Being entrepreneurial

Studied ☐

There are a lot of successful entrepreneurs in the business world who have identified a gap in the market or a need for a new product. Examples of entrepreneurs include:

- Tanya Budd and Hypo Hoist – Tanya was on a sailing course when she noticed that the 'man overboard' exercises did not work effectively; she designed a simple device with which to haul people out of the water.
- Mark Zuckerberg and Facebook – Mark introduced a computer site where people can chat with friends or find someone they have not seen for several years. Users have to register and set up a profile and can leave messages or talk to family and friends.
- Rose Grimond and Orkney Rose – Rose wanted people across the country to taste foods from family-run businesses in the Orkney Islands; she set up a business to deliver products to customers in different parts of the UK.
- Sergey Brin and Google – Sergey set up a research tool for searching for information on the internet. For a business Google can be used to investigate changes in trends, competitive activity and local business support.

Strong vision

Studied ☐

Any business will need a strong vision and someone who is prepared to follow through on their business idea:

- Alan Sugar – Lord Sugar started by selling electrical goods out of a van and then went on to set up Amstrad.
- Apple – an American company that made computer software and personal computers. Apple has remained successful because they have continued to review, adapt and develop their products.

Learning aim B: Plan an idea for a new business

Meeting customer needs

Studied ☐

It is important that any new or existing business knows their customers. A business needs to produce a product or service that meets the needs and expectations of their customers. To be successful a business will need to know what their customers want and when their products or services need to be adapted to meet customers' ever-changing expectations. Any new or existing business will need to know their main competitors and also any local businesses that sell similar products or services. It is important that the business knows their competitors' strengths and weaknesses, and how they can do better than their competitors.

Identifying new and changing needs

Studied ☐

Customers' needs change and it is important that a business is aware of how their needs and expectations have changed. There is a wide range of techniques for keeping up to date with what customers want; businesses can use methods such as conventional customer questionnaires, email surveys or social networking websites.

Continuing to meet established customer needs

Studied ☐

A business must keep aware of any developments in the products or services they sell. For a business to continue trading successfully they will want their customers to return for repeat purchases, so they must be aware when there is a gap in the provision they offer. A business must constantly review and evaluate the service they provide for their customers and identify whether there is still a market for the products or services they offer.

Measures of success

Studied ☐

For a business to remain profitable they must regularly review their procedures and processes. The business will need to review their:

- suppliers, for quality and price
- the control of income, expenditure and profits
- their reputation
- customer satisfaction
- competitors.

Business ideas

In this topic you will need to identify a gap or opportunity in the marketplace for a start-up business.

Researching the market and identifying gaps or opportunities

Studied ⬜

You should focus on the local area where you know the types of businesses and the products they sell. You will know the businesses that have been affected by the current volatile business environment and those that have remained strong.

Selecting a product or service

Studied ⬜

Knowledge of the local business environment is important when selecting a product or service you could use as a start-up business idea. You might, at first, come up with a few different ideas and then reject any business idea that you feel may not be successful.

Targeting customers

Studied ⬜

You may need support and guidance in choosing an appropriate and relevant business idea. When you have reached a decision on the product or service you will offer you will then need to identify your target markets; this will include:

- The age group of the target customers – is the product for the elderly, teenagers or children?
- The location for the business and why it is appropriate; for example, close to a busy bus station.
- Interests – why sell the product or service; for example, customers have identified a need for the product. Is there support from the local community for the introduction of the product or service?
- Concerns – what could go wrong and why.

Meeting the need or demand of targeted customers

Studied ⬜

You will need to explain and justify the need for your business and the product or service. Once you have decided on a business idea and the target market you will need to research the types of products your potential customers will want. You could use questionnaires or other research tools such as observations, sampling or test markets to investigate what customers want.

Features and benefits of the product or service

Look at the features of your product, including the characteristics of the product. For example, the feature could be a range of colours, sizes and shapes of teapots. You will also have to identify the benefits and advantages of the product. For example, the benefit of a binder would be to keep papers secure and tidy.

- Feature – you **describe** what it is.
- Benefit – you go on to **explain** what the feature will do for you.

A feature is of little or no use unless it has a benefit to the user. A car may have the *feature* of Bluetooth technology but this is only a *benefit* if someone has a mobile phone that they want to use in the car. A pair of shoes may have six-inch heels as a feature but this may not be a benefit if you are already more than six-feet tall.

A useful phrase to link these is: '…(feature)…which means that…(benefit)'.

Figure 1.6 These high heels will appeal to some customers, but not to others

Assessing the suitability of a business idea

Once you have identified a business idea and the target market, you will need to assess whether you have selected a suitable business idea.

Estimating resources

Studied

You will need to estimate the resources you require for the business idea. You should provide information on:

- the time required to investigate and research the local area
- the current skills you have for finance, marketing or administration
- areas of expertise such as ICT for administration or producing marketing materials
- attributes such as excellent communication skills for dealing with:
  - customers
  - any shortage of skills and where help is available
  - any support needed from a partner, and their skills and attributes
- where the financing to set up the business will come from; for example, your own money or a loan
- the location of the premises – should they be purchased or rented?
- the materials or resources required to make the product
- any equipment required, such as tables, chairs and a computer.

Figure 1.7 Your business may need premises, furniture and equipment

Selecting the most appropriate idea

Studied

You will need to assess the suitability of your business idea and whether you will have a market for the product or service. You may have chosen to focus on two business ideas and will have to make a decision on which idea is more appropriate or viable.

Likelihood of success or failure

Studied

Any business idea could succeed or fail; you should be able to explain why your business idea will be successful. You will need to provide evidence that you have researched the market and the target customer group to demonstrate a demand for your product. You should know your competitors and whether there is a demand for the product and how your product will be different from your competitors. And you will need to be certain you can get your products to your customers quickly and easily.

You will also need to estimate whether you expect to make a profit in the first year of trading or, if not, when you expect to be making a profit.

Barriers for a start-up business

Studied

You will need to identify any possible barriers for the start-up business. The barriers for the business could be any change in the business environment, such as an increase in interest rates that will impact on the repayment of loans, or that grants are not available in your area.

You will also need to consider any large start-up costs. Research may identify that some equipment is expensive and the only way forward would be to look at second-hand equipment.

You may require a special licence before you can start trading.

You may also identify that the competition is strong and has a monopoly on the local market and that you will not be able to compete with cheaper products.

Producing an initial plan for a business idea

To satisfy the requirements for this topic you will have to produce and submit an informative plan for your business idea.

Rationale

Studied ▢

The initial plan will need to justify why your business idea would be successful and be supported by any relevant research information. The initial plan should include the following evidence:

- The rationale and reasoning behind selecting the business idea
- The vision for the business – this could be to make a profit within one year of trading, to take a percentage of the market away from competitors or to become established in the marketplace
- The concept of the business and the product and why this business idea was selected and others were rejected.

Supporting evidence

Studied ▢

You should submit supporting evidence with your initial plan. You will need to identify clearly who your customers are likely to be (age group, niche, location and so on) and then, in the supporting evidence, there could be customer questionnaires identifying a need for the product. Similarly, you will identify how you will tell customers about the product and get the product to the customers – this must be realistic and in keeping with the product and the needs of the customers. For example, a product involving fresh food would need to be close to where customers live, whereas a product sold online only would not have that sort of restriction.

You should have decided on a strategy for dealing with competitors, such as undercutting their prices or the differentiation of your product.

Financing the business is one of the most important decisions to be made, and you should provide evidence on how you will raise the finance for the business. If the business is to be financed by a loan the supporting evidence should show investigation of the current interest rates as this will be a regular expense for the business.

Figure 1.8 Swimwear and water wings will sell better during the summer holidays

The decision on when to start the business may depend on the product or service but this could be to coincide with certain events. For example, if your product has a Christmas theme, such as an advent calendar, then it would be wise to set the business up in October/November when sales will be at their peak. A beachwear-based business should be up and running *before* the summer holidays.

Knowledge recap questions

1. List five things a potential business should consider before even starting to get going.

2. How would a business know it was successful?

3. Which of the following best describes how a start-up business should think?

    a. Benefits then work on the features

    b. Features then work on the benefits

    c. Features only

    d. Benefits only.

4. How would a business ensure that they continually meet the needs of their existing customers?

Assessment guidance for learning aim B

2B.P3 **Describe, using relevant examples, the features of successful businesses**

✍ Learner answer

A person wanting to set up a new business must identify a need for the product or service they want to offer. They could design a new product or make changes to existing products. Tanya Budd found the need for her Hypo Hoist, a man-overboard recovery system that recovers people from the sea. Dyson has improved vacuum cleaners to make them more effective. Budd and Dyson would have spent time and money investing in the development of their products.

Assessor report: The learner has identified why a new business would be set up and has given two very good examples of entrepreneurs (Tanya Budd and Dyson), but has not as yet **described** the features of a successful business. This means they need to give a clear description that includes all of the relevant features.

A business is successful if they know what their customers want and offer a good service. The business would need to know about their competitors and what they offer customers. Examples of successful businesses are NatWest, Dyson and Asda.

Assessor report: The learner has **outlined** two very important features of a successful business but has not **described** the features. They need to state why the features they have identified are important to the success of the business. The learner would need to describe why NatWest, Dyson and Asda are successful.

To be successful the business will need to know what customers want and provide a better service than their competitors. Asda sell a very good range of products for different types of customers and at lower prices than other supermarkets. Asda stays open late and provides extra services for customers, such as cafés, insurance, quick checkouts, cashpoints and discount vouchers. Asda now provides the opportunity for online shopping for busy workers and people who cannot leave their homes. Asda carry out customer surveys to see if they meet the needs of customers so that they can continue to make a profit.

Assessor report: The learner has described the features of why Asda is a successful business and should now complete the exercise for a different type of business.

Assessor report – overall

Is the evidence sufficient to satisfy the grading criterion?

The first part of the learner's evidence sets the scene and briefly outlines the reasons why a business is set up. The learner then outlines two important features of a successful business and then describes in more detail the features that make Asda a successful business. The learner has included brief comments on most of the points from the unit content. However, the learner has currently used only one example and the grading criterion for P3 does state 'businesses' and 'examples'.

What additional evidence, if any, is required?

The learner will need to describe the features of another successful business. It may be beneficial to focus on a different type of business.

Compare the features, strengths and weaknesses of two successful businesses

✍ **Learner answer**

	Asda	Dyson
Features	PLC Owned by Wal-Mart Wide range of products	PLC Owned in the UK High-quality products
Strengths	Price matching +10% difference Well known Late opening hours; some stores 24 hours Home deliveries as well as in-store shopping Online shopping Strong brand New stores opening New range of services such as insurance, holidays and credit cards	Different from other products because of the cyclone design Well-known brand of vacuum cleaner Regularly updates its products to stay ahead of the competition Online shopping and help Customer focused New products such as hand dryers and heaters
Weaknesses	Products not always available Own-label products are weak Online not available for all postcodes	Limited product range High price Maintenance is difficult and expensive Limited suppliers for spare parts

Assessor report: There is evidence that the learner has done some research about both Asda and Dyson but in the table the learner has simply **stated** facts about the businesses. Some of these facts could be **compared** as they have a common base, for example the range of products, but there is currently not enough development to achieve the merit grading criterion. **Comparing** means identifying the features, strengths and weaknesses of the two successful businesses and explaining the similarities and differences between them.

Both Asda and Dyson are PLCs, which means they are floated on the stock market and the general public can buy shares in them. However, Asda mainly sells products but does offer services such as insurance and credit cards, whereas Dyson needs shops to stock its products. You could buy a Dyson product at Asda.

Both businesses are aware of their customers and react to what they want. Asda offers a price promise and has opened extra hours; Dyson listened to its customers and brought out the 'Ball' as that's what customers wanted.

They are both well-known brands and are leaders in their fields. Asda has few real competitors as it's one of the 'big four' supermarkets. Dyson's main competitors are Vax, Miele, Bodner & Mann and Hoover. Asda has to be aware of what the others are doing; Dyson doesn't really as it has the brand name for this type of cleaner so some people will buy it anyway as they think it's the best one.

Asda, like Tesco, do home deliveries and customers can shop online. Customers can buy Dyson products online and their engineers will call out to fix a machine if it's still in warranty. Both offer good customer service. Asda has customer-service desks and will refund quickly if there is a problem; Dyson has experts on the phone to help with any questions. This means they are both trying to be the best in their market and they put the customer first so that they will come back and buy again.

With Asda home deliveries you cannot choose the actual product, so you might get something that is near to its sell-by date, which is a weakness.

Dyson products are expensive, so that is a weakness.

Both businesses are successful and making a profit, so they must be doing things right.

Assessor report: The learner has explained some good and valid points about Asda's and Dyson's strengths and has compared similarities. The comparisons are valid and well exemplified. However, the criterion requires a comparison of weaknesses as well as strengths. These have been mentioned but have not been covered in the same detail. Strengths and weaknesses require the same weighting and the learner would need to complete the comparison of weakness to ensure the criterion is met.

Assessor report – overall

Is the evidence sufficient to satisfy the grading criterion?

The table identifies some clear features and lists both strengths
and weaknesses but provides no comparison. The learner has used
some of the points identified in the table and compared the product
range, the competitors and how both businesses listen to customers'
needs. The evidence is insufficient for grading criterion M3 because
the learner has currently only focused on comparing features and
strengths and not weaknesses.

What additional evidence, if any, is required?

The learner will need to use the points from the table to compare the
weaknesses for Asda and Dyson.

Prepare a realistic initial plan for a business idea suitable for the local area

✍ **Learner answer**

My idea for a business is to make and sell bracelets and charms for mobile phones, iPods and handbags.

The bracelets will be made in a choice of different coloured beads and the charms will be just one or two coloured beads. Customers will be able to choose the colour of their beads and the products will be ready the same day.

Assessor report: The learner has identified their business idea and will now need to produce the supporting evidence.

I have produced a questionnaire to find out what bracelets and charms people at school and my family buy and the price they pay. My research shows that people would like the opportunity to buy bracelets and charms for lots of different reasons. I have looked at who my competitors are in the local area and where I can buy supplies. I only need to buy the beads, wire and some tissue paper, and can make them in my dad's garage.

Assessor report: The learner has identified how they did their research but will need to include a copy of the questionnaire. This can be put in an appendix to the report but needs to be available to be seen.

My competitors are Argos, a stall at the Saturday market, and people can buy charms online from a few different businesses. Argos only has a small choice of charms and not many different colours. I have got permission to open a stall before school and during lunch break for my enterprise project so I will be open five days a week. I will also be able to sell my charms during the enterprise days that take place at Easter, in the summer and at Christmas. I will also be able to sell them during the weekly craft fair at the town hall and at Sunday markets where my dad has a stall.

Assessor report: The learner has clearly researched the local area and identified their potential customers, routes to market and competitors. By noting the limit on what Argos sells, the learner has started to consider a strategy for dealing with the competition.

Assessor report – overall

Is the evidence sufficient to satisfy the grading criterion?

The learner has identified that there is a gap in the market because there are very few local competitors. However, to achieve the grading criterion the learner will need to demonstrate a need for the product and this will come from the results from the questionnaires.

What additional evidence, if any, is required?

The learner will need to include a copy of their questionnaire and a brief summary of the outcome.

(2B.M4) Explain how the initial plan for a business idea has the potential to respond to market needs

✍ Learner answer

My research shows that customers will buy my products and that there are very few competitors in the local area. My products are quick and easy to make and, because they are cheap but do not look cheap, they make good presents for family and friends or a small treat for anyone.

Assessor report: The learner has briefly identified why there is a potential market for the bracelets and charms but the command verb in the grading criterion is to **explain**. The learner will need to set out in detail, with reasons, how the initial plan for a business idea has the potential to respond to market needs.

People are buying charms to hang on their iPods, mobile phones, handbags, school bags, pencil cases and shoes. My research shows that people are buying charms for lots of different reasons and that they like the idea of being able to choose the colours to match bags, iPods, shoes or mobile covers. Because I am buying loose beads I will be able to let customers choose what size and colour beads they want. People will buy them because they can see what they are getting; if they buy from the internet they will not see the item before they buy.

My customers will be young people; they want to keep up with fashion and their friends so they will buy the latest items. People will buy my bracelets to match what they wear and this may mean that they have several different bracelets for their different clothes. People can choose the colour of the beads to match their different clothes.

If my business goes well I will look at opening a small shop or a market stall and I could think about employing other people.

Assessor report: The learner has provided a very good response and has **explained** why customers will buy the product. The learner has explained that customers will be able to choose the colour of their beads to match their outfits and how the reduced packaging will keep prices low. The learner has made no reference to their competitors and the impact this will have on their business idea.

Assessor report – overall

Is the evidence sufficient to satisfy the grading criterion?

The learner has explained how their initial plan for a business idea has the potential to respond to market needs, but to achieve M4 the learner will need to make some reference to their competitors. The learner will need to identify how their product will be differentiated from those offered by their competitors, and any difference in their pricing strategy. The learner should highlight how potential customers will benefit because of the limited choice offered by competitors and how purchasing online does incur costs for postage and packaging. The learner should also highlight why they can price their products lower than those of their competitors.

What additional evidence, if any, is required?

To achieve M4 the learner will need to add information about their competitors and explain why customers would buy the charms and bracelets they sell rather than those offered by their competitors.

Justify how the initial plan for a business idea has potential for success in relation to existing local businesses

✍ Learner answer

My research shows that one of my competitors, Argos, is over 8 miles from the school and customers have to pay £1.50 to park in the town centre. Argos only has a few to pick from and customers will not get to choose the colours they want. The charms and bracelets look good and are sold in coloured boxes.

My other main competitor is an outside stall at the local market. The stall is only open on Saturdays from 9 a.m. until 4.30 p.m., and the charms and bracelets are placed in large trays with other jewellery. The charms and bracelets are cheaper than Argos but do not look as good.

Charms 4 You is a family business that sells its charms online. Fab4crafts.com is another online business that sells kits to make your own charms with. There is a bigger choice of charms and bracelets for customers and they could be delivered the next day. To buy from online companies you have to pay postage unless you place a large order.

Assessor report: The learner has identified the competitors and described some of the similarities in the products they sell. The learner has not yet **justified** how their own business could be successful in relation to these existing local businesses. This means that they need to give reasons or evidence to support why they think their plan has the potential for success and show how they have arrived at this conclusion.

I will be selling my products at the school, which is a very large school close to a junior school and a home for elderly people. The children at the junior school come to all the enterprise events and so do the people in the home. The people in the home bring others to help them and they also buy goods. The sales at the enterprise events have always been good but I will need to do most of my selling at the weekend at the craft fair and at the market. I hope to sell lots of items at the school but I need to know that people will buy my charms and bracelets before I decide to open a shop or a stall.

At the craft fair and the market I hope to sell my charms and bracelets to lots of teenagers and young people, who all have iPods, handbags and mobile phones. I will have lots of different designs available in lots of different colours but will have different beads so I can make them how the customers want.

The charms and bracelets will look good and are for all age groups, not just teenagers. Mums and dads will be able to buy them as small treats or presents. Older people will buy them because they will want to keep up with fashion; my mum and her friends all like them.

Assessor report: The learner has identified the target consumer group and is starting to explain why people may buy their products. The learner will now need to justify how the business could be successful in relation to existing local businesses.

I have looked at where I can buy my beads and other materials. I could buy kits but they work out more expensive than buying all the beads, charms, wire and thread separately. There are a lot of companies that sell the materials online and I can get some good beads and charms on eBay. The beads, wire and thread will be the only items I have to buy. I can get tissues to wrap the charms from Poundland or Home Bargains for 59p.

There are a few stalls in the next town where they have a bigger outdoor and indoor market. The lady who runs one of the stalls is very good and will show you how to make the charms. The stalls are always busy and the lady said that she sells lots of charms to lots of different age groups. The lady said that people bought the made-up charms and bracelets rather than the loose beads and charms. The lady said it was easy to make the beads into charms and bracelets.

On Saturdays the other stalls are busy but on week days they are not always that busy. The lady on the bead stall said that she is very busy in the summer and at holiday times, and very, very busy at Christmas.

Assessor report: The work generated by the learner demonstrates that some research has been undertaken. The learner has identified how to get supplies and is beginning to make reference to the success of other local businesses. The learner has stated that companies sell materials online but should have given examples of these, for example a screenshot. The learner will need to identify how their product will be differentiated from the products sold at the markets.

Where I live lots of big shops have moved to the outlet centre and some shops are just left empty. Some small shops have opened in one part of the town – they are a cupcake shop, a kitchen café that just sells drinks and cakes, a newsagent and sweet shop, and a shop that sells things for babies. No one sells charms.

The Saturday market is always busy because customers want bargains, but that is just one day and there is only one stall that sells charms. There are no empty stalls but some people sell a lot of second-hand things and it does look like a boot fair, so the market is where people come looking to spend small amounts of money on something special but not expensive. As there is already a stall selling charms then they must sell, so I should do well as well. The market is not posh at all so my products will fit in OK. **a**

Local people, mostly older people, visit the craft fair at the town hall because the big posters say support local businesses. The local council gives a lot of support to new businesses and the mayor will open the shops and stalls. Again this gives me a head start because people know me and everyone likes to think they are helping locals, especially if I can sell them a product that is different from what they can buy at Argos. Also, people know that if they support me then I will buy things from them in return, so we all win. Everyone then feels proud of the local community, so we do well. It's like the Olympics and everyone on the same side. **a**

Assessor report: The learner has described some aspects of the current business environment for their local area but this does not justify totally why the business idea will be a success. However, the last two paragraphs in the answer do have comments that justify why the business should succeed. **a**

Assessor report – overall

Is the evidence sufficient to satisfy the grading criterion?

The learner has described the local competitors and the target consumer groups, and has briefly explained some aspects of the local business environment. The learner has set the scene but not yet reached a conclusion. The evidence submitted needs summarising and collating before the D2 grading criterion can be awarded.

What additional evidence, if any, is required?

The learner will need to add a paragraph that brings together all the points they have identified in each of the four sections evidenced. To achieve the D2 grading criterion the learner will need to summarise the main points and justify how the business could be successful in relation to existing local businesses.

Learning aim C
Present a business model for a business start-up

Assessment criteria

2C.P5 Explain the reasons for the choice of format selected for a business start-up.

2C.P6 Present a realistic business model for a business start-up.

2C.M5 Present a realistic business model for a business, explaining how the format and business model will enable it to carry out its activities successfully.

2C.D3 Present a realistic business model for a business, explaining how the format and supporting evidence justifies the initial business idea.

Learning aim C provides the opportunity for you to present your business idea. After compiling the information on trends and the current business environment, and how these may impact on a business and planning for the new business, you should present your business model.

Choice of format

You should investigate the different formats that are available and then choose the most appropriate one for your business idea. You will need to understand the features, advantages and disadvantages of each format.

Sole trader

Studied ☐

This is when just one person sets up a business. It is the easiest type of business to set up.

- There are several **advantages** of being a sole trader. The decisions are made by the owner and the owner will keep all the profits. There is very little administration required in setting up the business.
- The main **disadvantages** are that the owner is responsible if the business fails and for any claims from customers for accidents or faulty goods. If the owner is ill there may be no one to take over and the owner may have limited skills. After the initial start many sole traders cannot expand because they may have

46

limited money (capital) of their own to keep putting in and may not want to take out a loan. This may limit what the sole trader can do, even if demand is there.

Partnership

Studied ☐

A partnership is an agreement between two or more people to set up a business venture and is relatively easy to set up.

- The **advantages** of a partnership are that, because there is more than one person, it is easier to raise finance. The partners will be able to support one another and may have different skills and attributes that they can bring to the business. There will always be someone to discuss ideas with and to share the workload.
- The **disadvantages** are that the profits will have to be shared and each partner is liable for any bad decisions or any loss incurred. The main disadvantage of a partnership is unlimited liability, which means that each partner is liable for any debts. It may also take longer to make a decision because you have to consult the other partners and you may not always agree.

Limited company

Studied ☐

A limited company has shareholders who *own* the company; directors decide the strategy and managers put that strategy into operation. It means there are different stakeholders with different interests.

A limited company is a little more difficult to set up but this is because it allows the owners to keep their own finances and assets separate from the company.

Private limited company

A private limited company is usually medium-to-large in size and the shareholders (who are often the directors, too) want to keep their business separate from their personal interests and risks, so that if the business goes bust they only lose what they invest. They can only get money from private investors, usually people they know.

- The main **advantage** is the limited liability, but other **advantages** are that it is easy to raise finance and the business will have employees with more skills and attributes.
- The main **disadvantages** are that profits are shared and that decision making may take longer because more employees will be involved. Slow decision making may make it slower to respond to changes in the market.

Public limited company

A public limited company (PLC) is a large business that sells its shares on the stock market and is owned by the shareholders. A main difference with a private limited company is that the general public can buy shares in a PLC.

- The main **advantage** is that businesses can raise money easier and that they will employ people with specialist skills and knowledge.
- The **disadvantages** are that the profits are divided between the shareholders and that decisions are made by an elected board of governors.

Figure 1.9 An example of a public limited company

Social enterprises

Studied ☐

Social enterprises are set up to help support local communities, often in areas of high unemployment. The focus of these businesses is to make a profit and then to reinvest the profits back into the business.

- The main **advantage** of a social enterprise is that the business will create jobs in the local area and that government grants are available to support the business.
- The **disadvantage** is that they are more available in some locations than others and that the government could reduce funding and support.

Sources of help and support in developing a new business

Anyone starting up a new business will need to know where to go for help and advice. There is a wide range of organisations that provide new businesses with support and guidance.

Sources of help

Studied ☐

Financial support can come from banks, building societies or independent financial advisers. A financial adviser will provide guidance on start-up costs, loans to set up a business and investment, but this may be at a cost to the business.

Family members can be a good source of financial support as they are often keen to help out. They can buy 'shares' in the business but often do not want an early (or any) return. Getting and using finance from this source is often more flexible than entering into more rigorous arrangements with a bank.

Figure 1.10 Your bank is one possible source of finance

The Prince's Trust has many roles but one of their roles is to help support young people who want to set up a business that will benefit their local community.

Business Link provides support and guidance on a wide range of topics including starting up, grants and loans, and tax and VAT. Business Link has a very detailed and informative website.

Competitors' websites may provide information on products and pricing strategies.

Support networks

Studied

The Chamber of Commerce will provide support and advice for new business ideas and has several offices across the country and a useful website.

There are professional bodies such as accountants, who provide support on financial issues, VAT and taxes, and lawyers who will help with setting up the business, but both services will be a cost for the business.

Family and friends might already run a small business and they will be prepared to share information or to provide guidance, from their experiences, on what not to do.

The internet will identify any charities, voluntary organisations or trade organisations that provide support for businesses in your local area. A trade organisation will provide support and advice on their relevant markets and products.

Business model

Definition of a business model

You need to present a clear definition of a business model and identify how the business aims to make a profit. The business model will identify the product, the income and expenditure for the business and the profit margin. The model should include all of the running costs for the business such as rent, materials and advertising, and any start-up costs such as a loan. The model will need to identify the revenue; this could be in format of a simple pricing strategy for the business.

Components of a business model

The components of a business model will need to include:

- The outcome of any market research including research on current trends, the needs and expectations of potential customers, information on suppliers and competitors.
- Information on the goods or services the business is planning to offer. The model should identify if the business is buying materials to make a product or planning to just buy a product and sell it on for a profit.
- The business aims or long-term goals. The model could highlight any plans for future development such as advertising or selling online.
- The main business objectives, outlining any measurable targets such as 'to make a 10 per cent profit within 12 months'. Any targets should be SMART (specific, measurable, achievable, realistic and time-related).
- The stakeholders of the business – the business model will need to identify the format of the business and its owners. If the business is a sole trader how will the business be financed or, if a partnership, how will decisions be made. These are the main stakeholders but there may be others too, such as:
  - employees, who want the business to succeed in order to keep their jobs
  - customers, who want to keep well supplied and will monitor quality
  - investors, such as a bank who will need to know its money is well used and that it will get it back with interest
  - competitors, who will be interested to see how the new business affects them.

- Finance – for example, whether the business incurred any costs for start-up. The business model should identify how the business was financed and any start-up costs, such as equipment or premises.
- Information on how the products will be sold to customers – whether from a fixed location such as a shop or from a mobile van or online. If products are to be sold online it would be beneficial to identify any additional costs, such as postage and packaging. Some products or services lend themselves to franchising, where other people buy the right to sell the product in their own area but leave the advertising and product development to the original company. Other products or services lend themselves to direct selling, often by way of product 'party plans' where they can showcase what they have to offer in customers' homes or workplaces.
- Finally, evidence to justify why the business idea will succeed in the local area. This should include any supporting evidence that identifies a need for the business.

Figure 1.11 Stakeholders

Figure 1.12 A local business like this needs to meet a real need among local customers

Knowledge recap questions

1. How do shares in a limited company differ from a PLC?

2. Put the following features under the correct business format in the table: unlimited liability, limited liability, company provides all the training for you, take holidays when you want, only sell what the company says you can, has a board of directors

Sole trader	Limited company	Franchise

3. Explain, with an example, what limited liability means.

4. Match the following stakeholders in a PLC with the correct description: shareholders, directors, managers

They set the aims and objectives of the business, then the strategy to achieve these	
They run the business on a day-to-day basis	
They invest in the business in the hope of making a profit	

5. All businesses have aims and objectives. What is the difference between aims and objectives? Give two examples of each to show your understanding.

6. A gap in the market has been spotted to process waste from farms in a village. The local community and the bank are stakeholders in this possible business. Explain their interest.

Assessment guidance for learning aim C

2C.P5 **Explain the reasons for the choice of format selected for a business start-up**

✍ Learner answer

I am going to set up as sole trader called Carole's Charms (CC) because it is easiest and it suits my business.

Assessor report: This is just a statement and does not **explain** why this format is suitable or any knowledge of other formats. Explaining means that they have to set out in detail the reasons for the choice of format. It is helpful to give an example to show what you mean when explaining – start by introducing the topic, then give the 'how' or 'why'.

I have decided to set up as a sole trader rather than a franchise or a limited company or even a partnership (which I thought about) because I want to keep all the profits myself. **a**

Assessor report: This is a better start and has given a partial explanation about why a format was chosen, **a** but it does not **explain** any knowledge of the **characteristics** of the other types of format. There is still not sufficient evidence for grading criterion P5.

I looked at whether I should get a franchise for my product as they had the 'name' for this sort of thing and they would do the advertising. I also thought of going into partnership with my friend as she is really good at paperwork and is organised so we'd make a good team with different skills. A limited company would have been no use to me as the business is just starting and I don't want to have other people involved, even though I'd have a limit on the amount of money I could lose. **b**

Assessor report: The learner has started to focus on other formats and provided some good information on their characteristics. They have explained why a limited company would not be a suitable format for their own business, **b** but have not done this when discussing the franchise or the partnership they considered.

Assessor report – overall

Is the evidence sufficient to satisfy the grading criterion?

The learner has only identified one reason for their chosen format **a** and will need to explain in more detail why they have chosen to trade as a sole trader rather than the other formats. There is still not sufficient evidence for grading criterion P5.

What additional evidence, if any, is required?

To achieve grading criterion P5 the learner will need to explain, with examples, why they have chosen to trade as a sole trader and why the other formats are not appropriate for their business.

Present a realistic business model for a business start-up

✍ Learner answer

This is my business model:

- I will set up as a sole trader.
- I will make the bracelets and charms in my dad's garage.
- My competitors are Argos, the local market stall and some web-based companies.
- I have done some research and people said they would buy my products mainly because there was no other local business like mine.
- I've got enough money to start up the business and run it because I only need to buy the beads, thread, wire and some tissues.
- I think I can make a profit by the end of one year.

My marketing plan is:

- Price – just a bit less than Argos and the market stall in town.
- Place – I will sell my products at school, craft fairs and maybe set up a website.
- Promotion – I will advertise around school and I will get local fairs to include me on their list of traders.
- Product – custom-made beads and charms for iPods, mobiles, handbags and shoes; bead bracelets in lots of colours.

Assessor report: The learner has made a good start and has identified the main elements of a business model. The learner will now just need to present these points in a little more detail to achieve grading criterion P6.

CC is the name of my business and I will be sole trader as it's the easiest and cheapest way to set up, plus I get all the profits and I work when I want to. I'll be making bracelets and charms mainly for iPods and mobile phones, but I will also make them to order, especially coloured ones, if people want them. I can do this because I'm a sole trader and I make the decisions.

I researched my friends and did a local poll of people I didn't know and they all said the bracelets and charms would sell. I thought my friends might just be being nice so that's why I asked the other people. There are some websites selling this sort of thing so that was my secondary research that told me they would sell.

The competition is Argos and the local market stall. They are both bigger than me but they only sell what they get – I can make individual stuff. My dad will let me make the charms and bracelets in his garage. **a** I can buy the beads, thread and wire on eBay to start with and tissues for wrapping for 59p from Home Bargains. This means I can keep all the profit. I will price my charms about 10 per cent less than Argos, so they're cheaper but don't seem cheap. I will sell them at breaks and lunchtimes at school from a table and I will also do the weekly craft fair at the town hall and at Sunday markets where my dad has a stall. This is also free, so I don't have any unnecessary costs.

I will create some posters to put up around school and at the fairs. Again, these will be just about free, so I don't owe anyone anything I can't afford if sales are slow. My objective is to survive for six months and make a profit after 12 months when people get to know me better.

Assessor report: The learner has added more detail to most of the points listed in the first section of their evidence but will need to add more detail for all points. For example, the learner has restated that they will make the bracelets in their dad's garage **a** but should have added some more detail about this, such as the rent and overhead costs involved with this, and any general start-up costs.

Assessor report – overall

Is the evidence sufficient to satisfy the grading criterion?

In the first part of their answer the learner has identified the main elements of a business model and their marketing ideas. In second part of the learner's work they have gone on to develop some of the points in more detail. They would need to do this for all points for there to be sufficient evidence for grading criterion P6.

What additional evidence, if any, is required?

The learner needs to add some further detail for all points, including about making the charms in their dad's garage.

2C.M5 Present a realistic business model for a business, explaining how the format and business model will enable it to carry out its activities successfully

✍ Learner answer

My business will be successful because being a sole trader is better for me than being in a partnership or a limited company of some sort. I want to make a profit so I will not be a social enterprise. Being a sole trader means I can make all the decisions and keep all the profit. That sort of suits my character.

I did some research and decided my idea for CC would work. There is not much competition so I should do OK, especially as I can sell direct to the customer, which will give me an advantage.

I aim to be successful and make lots of money. To start with I don't want to be greedy, so I just want to make about 10 per cent profit in the first year.

Like I said earlier, I don't have a lot of overheads as my dad will help me out, so that is good and gives me an advantage over other businesses selling the same goods. People at the craft fairs and market will like my products as it will bring more people to their stalls as well.

Overall, because I'm starting small and I'm running things, and I don't owe anybody anything, I think my business will be very successful.

Assessor report: This is currently just a statement of decisions made earlier in the assignment and does not **explain** why this format is more suitable than other formats. This means they need to set out in detail, with reasons, why the format is more suitable than other formats. The learner has taken the sections of a business model and made some **outline** comments only, none of which are really supported with an explanation as to how they will enable it to carry out its activities successfully. This is not sufficient evidence for grading criterion M5.

Having looked at various formats I have decided to be a sole trader. There are good reasons for this. I get to make all the decisions about what to sell and where to sell, so I am controlling what is happening. This would not happen with a partnership as I would have to agree things with my partner(s) and this might be difficult. **a** I don't want to buy a franchise or be a limited company. **b**

There is less risk in being a sole trader as I don't have to spend money on buying a franchise or paying for special premises if I was a limited company, or having to pay for an accountant to keep my money right. If it doesn't work I can just walk away. There is sort of a greater risk because I can get sued for everything I own but, because my beads are cheap, the risk is really small. **a**

As a sole trader I get to decide what I do and when and how. I don't have to ask for approval and I can make decisions quickly, which can't happen with the other formats. **a**

All my research shows that I'll be a success by selling locally, and because my dad is helping (to keep costs down) it means all the money goes to me so – unless I sell nothing – then I will do very well. If I do very well I will expand and maybe take someone on work experience to help me.

Assessor report: This is an example of an excellent start and the learner has covered the format element very well, explaining why it will enable them to carry out their business activities successfully. **a** The learner has rejected franchise and limited company status but needs to give reasons why they have rejected them **b** – why those formats are not suitable for what the start-up business needs now.

Unfortunately the evidence to cover the business model is too sparse. The learner should be encouraged to expand on the evidence generated and submitted for grading criterion P6. The learner has noted that they want to start off part time, local, very small, doing it all themselves, control of everything from producing to selling, minimal risk with finance and so on, all elements that point strongly towards being a sole trader to get the business up and running. The other formats would suit other types of business and may be a thought for this business in the future.

Assessor report – overall

Is the evidence sufficient to satisfy the grading criterion?

The learner has focused more on the format of the business than the model. The learner has explained why their chosen format is more appropriate for their business and why other formats were rejected. The learner will need to develop their evidence and explain how their business model will enable the business to be successful. They will need to do this to generate sufficient evidence for grading criterion M5.

What additional evidence, if any, is required?

To achieve grading criterion M5 the learner will need to develop the points identified in P6. The learner will need to explain why the chosen model will enable the business to be successful.

✍ Learner answer

I am setting my business, CC, up as a sole trader. I will be a small business and when I looked at the advantages and disadvantages for each format I decided a sole trader would be best. There are few start-up costs, I don't have to share with anyone, I can work when I want, sell what I want, and even stop when I want to. If it all goes wrong then there's only me to answer to. The other formats are more complicated and I might have to send in accounts (limited company), or I can only sell what they let me and then I have to pay them some of the profits(franchise), or I might end up not getting on with the other people so we'd go bust (partnership). As a sole trader I will be my own boss and make all the decisions and keep all the profits. **a**

Assessor report: The learner has developed the points they identified for M5 and has **justified** why the format of a sole trader is the most appropriate format for their business. **a** This means they have given reasons why it is most appropriate and shown how they have arrived at this conclusion. The learner will now need to justify and evaluate why they feel their business will be successful. They should compare their business venture with existing businesses.

My aim is to survive for the first six months then make a profit after 12 months, and then I will decide on whether to continue as I am or to rent a shop and make more charms. I will need to look at what customers want because charms may not be the thing to buy. The lady on the market stall says that her stall is doing good business and there are more and more websites selling charms, so I should be OK.

Assessor report: The learner has explained what their plans are for the future and has correctly identified that consumers' taste may change so they need to review the market. The learner has made some link to the growth in demand for charms in the local area but has not identified that additional websites mean an increase in competition.

I should be OK as there are no overheads to pay at school, the fair, the market or for my dad's premises, so that means any money I get I can keep (apart from buying the bead themselves), so if I don't sell much I don't have a massive loss for the day and it's no big deal. I don't need any grants or loans as I only have to buy the beads and I can afford them myself – so again, I don't owe anybody anything.

I have looked at how to buy the beads, wire and thread and have decided to buy in bulk from the stall in the next town. If I buy from a website I will get the beads cheaper but will not get to see the beads and I will have to pay for postage, which is £5.50, and this will make the cost £58.00.

Assessor report: The learner has explained why the business overheads are low and has investigated the most appropriate way to buy the materials. The learner has said they will buy locally and has found out the prices online, which is good, but they should have included how much the stall in the next town was charging to compare with the online prices to justify why they decided to buy from the stall in the next town.

My research shows that there is not much competition and it is mostly from Argos – a big company. They have a different format so, although they can advertise better than me, they cannot change the products or the prices quickly as they have to wait for head office to tell them. I can respond to local market needs, for example customising charms in school colours or using their logo. I will not be using boxes or packages so my charms and bracelets will be cheaper and better for the environment. I am just using cheap tissues for wrapping so there is not very much waste or things to throw away.

Web-based companies are no problem as it's only a cheap product and people would prefer to 'feel' and see them before they buy, and they have to pay postage. The charms could get broken in the post and you would have to return them and then wait for more.

The market stalls sell beads and things but not many are made into charms or bracelets, so the customer would have to make them. I am selling charms and bracelets at a good price and the customer can choose the beads and wear them or use them straight away. If I am not busy I will make the charms for the customer to take away or do them while they do their shopping. The longest anyone will wait is one day.

My other research shows that local people want to buy my charms because they're cheap, they're personal, they're fashionable and because I'm local – and people want to support local businesses if they can. So again, short term at least, I should do OK. It might happen that someone else soon starts to do the same thing so that might affect me, but not to start with.

Assessor report: The learner has explained how their product is different from the local competition and has justified why they can keep prices low, because of the reduced packaging and no postal costs.

I will not have to pay for advertising because I will design posters at school in art and on the computer in my ICT and enterprise lessons. The posters will go up at school and I will take some to the fair and market stall. I will do some price charts on the computer and ask my dad to laminate them so I will not to pay. The school magazine does bits on people who are doing things for enterprise; this is sent home each term so I will be able to tell mums and dads about my charms.

At the town hall there is a man who does big posters for all the stalls and he said that they are free because the council wants more stalls to open. I will not have to pay for the posters and I get to say what I want on them.

Assessor report: The learner has explained how and where they will advertise and how they can advertise at no cost to the business.

So, with little risk – easy to get away from the business if it goes wrong; few competitors in the first place; my dad's help with premises and making the charms; a classy, catchy name like CC; various different local places to sell to and different target markets; somebody else doing the advertising (craft fairs) and me doing the adverts for nothing at school – I should succeed and the whole thing fits together very well.

Assessor report: This is a good response and the learner has taken into account the advantages and disadvantages of different formats and explained and justified most steps of the business model.

Assessor report – overall

Is the evidence sufficient to satisfy the grading criterion?

The learner has explained and presented their business format and model. The learner has justified how their business idea could be a success in most places and how it is differentiated from its local competitors. Although the learner is submitting this evidence for grading criterion D3, the evidence is sufficient to satisfy grading criterion M5. There may be times when a learner will produce work that covers all or part of a grading criterion 'by accident'. To achieve D3, they will need to ensure they have justified all parts of the supporting evidence.

What additional evidence, if any, is required?

The learner needs to justify all parts of the supporting evidence, including why they have chosen to buy their beads, wire and thread at the local stall. They could have included evidence of their research with their work. The learner could have delivered the evidence for grading criterion D3 in a slideshow presentation as a sales pitch, for example.

Model assignment: UNIT I Enterprise in the business world, learning aim A

PROGRAMME NAME:	BTEC Level 2 First Award in Business
ASSESSOR:	
DATE ISSUED:	SUBMISSION DATE:
INTERIM REVIEW:	INTERIM REVIEW:

This assignment will assess the following learning aim and grading criteria:

A Know how trends and the current business environment may impact on a business.

2A.P1 Outline how the business environment can impact on a start-up business.

2A.P2 Explain how current trends will impact on a start-up business.

2A.M1 Explain how changes in the current business environment are likely to impact on a start-up business.

2A.M2 Compare how two trends have impacted on a start-up business.

2A.D1 Assess the current risks, opportunities and trends in the business environment for a start-up business.

Scenario

You have just submitted the final part of your coursework and have decided that the time is right for you to start up your own business. You have decided on an idea for your business and your first task is to research the business environment and current trends to find out how they will impact on your business idea.

You will need to produce a leaflet that outlines how the business environment and current trends will impact on your business. Please remember to keep a list of any websites, journals, newspapers or books you have used.

Task 1

The first part of your leaflet is an **outline** of how the business environment can impact on your business idea. Your leaflet should include information on:

- national factors, such as the economy and taxation
- local factors, such as competitors and suppliers.

You will need to **explain** how **any changes** in the current business environment will have an impact on your business idea.

Task 2

The next part of your leaflet is to explain how current trends will impact on your business idea. You will need to include information on:

- social trends
- technology trends
- environmental trends
- ethical trends.

Choose **two** of the trends and **compare** how they have impacted on a local start-up business. Please select a business that you know well and compare **both** the similarities and the differences.

Task 3

The final section of your leaflet is to **assess** the current risks, opportunities and trends in the business environment that will affect your business idea. You will need to demonstrate that you have researched current sources of information and highlight how you have reached your decisions.

Please remember to identify any websites, journals, newspapers or books you have used.

Model assignment: UNIT 1 Enterprise in the business world, learning aims B and C

PROGRAMME NAME:	**BTEC Level 2 First Award in Business**
ASSESSOR:	
DATE ISSUED:	SUBMISSION DATE:
INTERIM REVIEW:	INTERIM REVIEW:

This assignment will assess the following learning aim and grading criteria:

B Plan an idea for a new business.

(2B.P3) Describe, using relevant examples, the features of successful businesses.

(2B.P4) Prepare a realistic initial plan for a business idea suitable for the local area.

(**2B.M3**) Compare the features, strengths and weaknesses of two successful businesses.

(**2B.M4**) Explain how the initial plan for a business idea has the potential to respond to market needs.

(**2B.D2**) Justify how the initial plan for a business idea has potential for success in relation to existing local businesses.

This assignment will also assess the following learning aim and grading criteria:

C Present a business model for a business start-up.

(2C.P5) Explain the reasons for the choice of format selected for a business start-up.

(2C.P6) Present a realistic business model for a business start-up.

(**2C.M5**) Present a realistic business model for a business, explaining how the format and business model will enable it to carry out its activities successfully.

(**2C.D3**) Present a realistic business model for a business, explaining how the format and supporting evidence justifies the initial business idea.

Learning aim C: Present a business model for a business start-up

Scenario

There is a lot of local interest in your business and you have been asked to produce a PowerPoint presentation for local investors. You will need to prove to potential investors that you understand what makes a business successful. The potential investors will also need information about your product, the format of the business; your finance and how you can justify that your business will be successful.

Please remember that you will need to submit the notes to support your presentation and to keep a list of any websites, journals, newspapers or books you have used.

Your teacher/assessor will produce an observation statement to support your presentation, research information and presentation notes.

Task 1

The first part of your presentation is to **describe** the features of three successful businesses. You will need to describe why the businesses you have chosen are successful.

The next part of your presentation will be to **compare** the features, strengths and weaknesses for two of the businesses you have researched.

Task 2

The third section of your presentation is to put forward your business idea for the local area. You need to prepare a realistic initial plan, which will include information on:

- the product
- resources; sources of finance, equipment, employees, your skills
- potential customers
- competitors
- marketing plan.

You will now need to add information to your presentation that explains how your initial plan has the potential to respond to market needs.

Will your business idea work? In this part of your presentation you will need to **justify** how your business idea has the potential for success in relation to existing local businesses.

Task 3

The next part of your presentation is to **explain** which type of ownership format you have selected for your business idea and why. You should explain why the format you have chosen is more appropriate than other formats.

You will now need to present a realistic business model for your business idea. You will need to include information on the following in order to complete the model:

- the name of your business
- how customers can buy from your business
- the aims and objectives of your business
- stakeholders
- finance and start-up costs
- results of market research you have carried out
- the support available for a new business like yours.

The next part of your presentation will need to **explain** how your chosen format and business model will enable you to carry out the activities successfully. You will need to give reasons why the format and model are more suitable for your business than other formats or models.

The final part of your presentation is to explain how the format and supporting evidence justifies the need for your business idea. You will need to **justify** why your business idea could be successful and how it responds to market needs. You could, if relevant, compare your business idea to existing businesses.

Please remember to include information on where you did your research, the notes to support your presentation and the observation document completed by your teacher/assessor.

UNIT 2
Finance for business

Unit 2, Finance for Business, is a core unit and the only externally assessed unit for the BTEC Level 2 First Award in Business qualification. You are assessed through sitting an on-screen test.

The Finance for Business unit introduces you to the costs incurred by a business during both the initial start-up phase and when trading. You will investigate the ways a business will generate revenue and how you can calculate profit.

This section of the assessment guide is divided into two main sections. The first section focuses on guidance for the three learning aims for this unit. All of the topics in the learning aims should be covered in the delivery of the qualification.

The second section provides guidance and examples for the on-screen test. The test will last for one hour and is a mix of questions, including questions requiring a short explanation. It is important that any relevant formulae are learnt because they may not be recorded on the test documents. If a question requires some calculations it is always beneficial to show the working out because, even if the final answer is incorrect, there may be marks awarded for using the correct formula. The book contains two question papers, each with 19 questions and a total of 50 marks. The marks awarded for each question or part of a question are clearly shown in bold and in brackets. The answers for each question paper are provided at the end of the book.

Learning aim A
Understand the costs involved in business and how businesses make a profit

Learning aim A covers the different types of costs involved with setting up and running a business, as well as how revenue is generated and how to calculate profit.

Understand the costs involved in business

This topic focuses on the costs involved with running a business.

Start-up costs

It takes a lot of money to set up and run a business and there will be several items to buy before the business can open the door to customers. The start-up costs for a business may include:

- raising money to set up the business – for example, a loan
- premises – shop, office or garage
- fitting out the premises – shelves, decorating, cupboards
- equipment – tables, chairs, machines, tills, telephones
- transport – car, van
- materials and/or resources – raw materials to make products
- payments for lawyers or accountants
- advertising – posters or adverts in newspapers
- insurance – for buildings, equipment
- utilities – connection of gas, electricity and water
- licence – may be needed to sell certain goods or services.

Operating (running) costs

When the business is up and running there will still be costs that are incurred in the day-to-day running of a business. The operating costs will include:

- rent or mortgage
- restocking of materials
- wages for employees
- interest on any money borrowed
- utility bills – gas, electricity and water
- telephone and internet
- repairs and maintenance
- insurance.

Fixed and variable costs

Studied ☐

A business will incur two types of costs – fixed costs and variable costs – and it is important to identify which cost falls into which category.

- **Fixed costs** are costs that remain the same even when sales fall or increase. Fixed costs are costs such as rent, insurance and loan repayments.
- **Variable costs** are costs that will rise when the sales increase and fall when there is a fall in the demand for the product. Examples of variable costs are materials, electricity and wages. If a business needs to save money they will look at reducing their variable costs.

Direct and indirect costs

Studied ☐

Any business will need to know the difference between direct and indirect costs.

- **Direct costs** are the costs that can be linked to a product, such as the raw materials and labour used to make it.
- **Indirect costs** are often called overheads and are costs that are relevant for the business to operate but which are not directly linked to a specific product. Indirect costs include costs such as advertising, furniture and cleaning materials.

In some businesses, such as a sole trader, variable costs will be the same as direct costs; and fixed costs the same as indirect costs.

Total costs

Studied ☐

The total costs are the sum of all the costs needed to run a business. So the total costs are all the fixed costs and all the variable costs. The total costs are important in helping the owners of a business decide on how much they must charge for their products so that they can make a profit.

The calculation for the total costs is:

total costs = fixed costs + variable costs

Understand how businesses make a profit

This topic focuses on how the business will generate revenue and on how to calculate profit.

Revenue

Studied ☐

A business will make money – generate income – from selling their products or services to customers. The more products the business sells, the more money they will make.

The revenue for a business will generally come from the sale of their products or services to customers.

To calculate the revenue the business will need to know how many products were sold and the price the customer paid for each product. The formula is:

revenue = number of sales × price per unit

For example, if a business sold 780 products at a price of £8 per unit, the revenue is:

£6,240 (revenue) = 780 (products sold) × £8 (price per unit)

Expenditure

Studied ☐

A business will have to spend money to set up the business and to buy or rent premises. The business will need to purchase equipment and materials to produce the products they will sell to customers. If a business is providing a service rather than a product they will need equipment, such as computers, hardware and software, desks, chairs and telephones. The business will also need to pay for the use of gas, electricity and water (utilities). The business may employ staff and will have to pay wages. There will also be costs incurred for any advertising and for getting professional advice from an accountant or lawyer.

Expenditure is any payment the business will have to make to run the business.

Overheads are the daily costs incurred when running a business. Overhead expenses include rent or mortgage; utility bills for gas, electricity, water, telephone and internet; wages and materials used to make the product; and repairs.

Types of expenditure, including overheads:

- premises – rent or mortgage payments
- materials and resources
- equipment and repair costs
- utility bills for the use of gas, electricity and water
- transport – purchase, tax, insurance, MOT, repairs
- wages
- telephone and internet – connection and rental
- advertising and administration
- insurance
- professional advice – accountant, lawyer.

Calculating profit and loss

It is important for a business to know how much money they have coming in – revenue – and how much they have to pay out – expenditure. The business will need to know that they have sufficient money coming in so that they can pay their bills.

When a business generates more money in revenue than they have to pay out on expenditure, they will make a profit. The business will have sufficient money to pay for its overheads and some money for investing.

When a business does not have sufficient money from the revenue to cover their expenditure, they will make a loss. The business will not have sufficient money to pay for its overheads.

The business will be able to calculate its profit by subtracting the total expenditure from the total for revenue:

profit = revenue – expenditure

Learning aim B
Understand how businesses plan for success

Learning aim B provides the opportunity to learn how to calculate breakeven and to identify if the business is making a profit or a loss. It also focuses on the importance of budgeting and cash flow forecasting.

Understand the planning tools businesses use to predict when they will start making a profit

This topic focuses on breakeven analysis and how to calculate breakeven.

Breakeven

Studied ☐

Breakeven is when the business has made sufficient revenue to pay their overheads but there is nothing left over. This is when revenue and expenditure are the same; there is no profit and no loss. For example, if the business made £5,000 in revenue and the total costs to produce and sell the products were £5,000 then the business is breaking even: no profit, no loss.

To calculate breakeven a business will need to know the fixed costs, the variable cost and the price for each product unit sold. Breakeven analysis will help the business determine its margin of safety: this is how a business can analyse where they can still make a profit if there was a fall in sales or how much costs could increase before the business was making a loss.

A business can produce a breakeven chart that will show the following:

- breakeven point (the amount of sales needed to cover costs)
- profit – money left after all costs have been paid
- loss – insufficient money to pay the overheads and bills
- variable costs – linked to the number of products produced
- fixed costs – items such as premises and equipment that remain constant
- total revenue – income for the business
- total costs – fixed and variable costs
- margin of safety – the excess units produced beyond the breakeven point.

The breakeven point can be calculated by the following formula:

$$\text{breakeven} = \frac{\text{fixed costs}}{\text{selling price per unit} - \text{variable cost per unit}}$$

For example, if fixed costs are £400, the price per product is £60 and the variable cost per product is £20, then:

$$\text{breakeven is } 10 = \frac{400}{60 - 20}$$

Breakeven is important for all businesses because it identifies how many products they will need to sell to cover all business expenditure. If the business is not selling the sufficient number of products to achieve the breakeven point it will be making a loss. Once the business reaches the breakeven point it will be making a profit.

If the business is not making sufficient revenue to pay its bills it will need to look at making changes or it will go into debt and maybe even have to close.

The following information has been used to produce the breakeven chart:

- Fixed costs = £400
- Variable costs per unit = £80
- Revenue (selling price) per unit = £120

The breakeven point is when revenue and total costs are both £1,200.

The breakeven chart highlights that 11 units must be sold before the business will make a profit. At ten units the business is not making a profit or a loss.

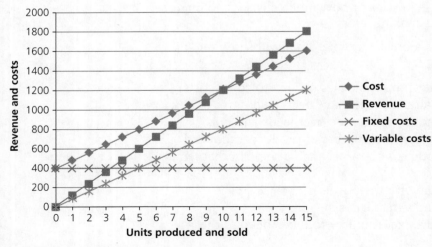

Figure 2.1 The breakeven chart

The business can change the figures in the breakeven analysis to investigate what impact different scenarios would have on the profit margin. The business could change the fixed or variable costs to calculate how many more products would be needed to break even or make a profit.

If the breakeven analysis identifies that there is insufficient revenue to cover the costs, the business could look at increasing the price of the products or look at ways to reduce its spending. If the business decided to reduce its spending it could look for cheaper suppliers, look at ways to reduce spending on utility bills, wages or even look for cheaper premises.

If there was an increase in fixed costs or variable costs the business would need to sell more products to make a profit or, again, look at ways to reduce the costs.

Limitations of breakeven charts

Studied ☐

It is important to understand that a breakeven chart is not an exact representation of exactly when a business will move into profit. On the breakeven chart for CC jewellery it was estimated that, on average, bracelets are sold regularly. In reality, most customers will only come in for different items as and when they are needed. This would change the revenue figures being achieved and the breakeven point would be different. It is, however, a very useful guide and is easy to understand.

Understand the tools businesses use to plan for success

This topic looks at the purpose of setting budgets and how to produce a cash flow forecast.

Budgeting

Studied ☐

A budget is a plan for the future and identifies how the business plans to spend its revenue and how any expenditure will be financed. A budget is an effective way to plan both the revenue and expenditure. Budgeting will identify if the business can just continue as it is or whether it needs to review sales or costs. Budgeting will identify if the business is in a position to make changes or expand.

An expenditure budget is an **estimate** of all the planned business costs for a set period of time. The expenditure budget will need to include estimates for any changes the business is planning to make, such as the purchase of new equipment.

A revenue budget will **estimate** how much money the business will expect or want to make from sales over a set period of time. The revenue budget is just a forecast of what the business would like to make and, when planning any changes, the business will need to consider the current business environment.

Budgetary control

Studied ☐

The budget is the plan for what the business wants to achieve in the future; budgetary control is the review of whether the business has achieved its goals. The budgetary control will compare the business's actual performance against the planned target performance and, when the business has not achieved its planned targets, it may need to take corrective actions. The budgetary control process will help the business achieve its objectives.

Cash flow forecasting

Studied ☐

Any business will need money to pay its bills and it is important that it knows when and how much money is coming in. It is important that a business knows it will have sufficient money coming in to cover its outgoings – outflows such as suppliers or wages. A business will want to be in a position where it has more money coming into the business than it has going out.

The cash flow forecast will record and identify the source of the money coming in each month and the money going out each month, and whether there is any excess money at the end of the month. A negative balance is usually shown in red or in brackets.

The cash flow forecast will also record the bank balance at the start and end of the period.

Inflows

Inflows are money that is coming into the business. Examples of inflows are:

- capital – money paid in to set up the business
- money from selling products or services to customers
- loans
- overdrafts
- interest paid on savings.

An inflow is actual money and does not include any money that is owed by customers to the business.

Outflows

Outflows are money going out of the business. Examples of outflows are:

- rent or mortgage for premises
- wages for employees
- purchase of stock or materials from suppliers
- utility bills such as gas, electricity and water
- telephone and internet
- advertising, which may not be each month
- repairs
- purchase of new equipment
- insurance
- repayment on loans.

Some of the outflows will be the same amount each month and will be paid on the same day, such as loan repayments, rent or mortgage.

Figure 2.2 Money flows out of this business to pay for the computers, staff wages and the phone and electricity bills

Timing of inflows and outflows

A business will always need to know that it has sufficient money to pay its everyday bills such as suppliers or staff wages. Without materials and staff the business will not be able to produce the products to sell to the customers and there will be no money coming into the business.

The business must ensure that the timing of incoming money is efficient so that there is always sufficient money available to pay for day-to-day business costs. It is important that customers pay their bills and that they pay on time. Late payments from customers will mean insufficient money to pay the business costs and could result in no money to pay for materials, utility bills or loan repayments. Any late payments for bank loans could mean an increase in the interest owed, while late payments to suppliers may result in no raw materials.

Using the cash flow forecast to plan for business success

Studied

If the cash flow forecast identifies that a business will have a large sum of money just sitting in the bank it should look at investing the money to make interest for the business.

A cash flow forecast will enable a business to find out if it will have sufficient surplus to invest in new resources or equipment, or whether it can expand the business. The forecast will highlight months when the income from sales will not be sufficient to cover the outgoings and the business can then decide what to do. With this information the business can decide what steps to take; the business may decide that it needs to increase the price of its products, look for cheaper suppliers or change the months when it pays quarterly bills. The cash flow forecast may highlight that there is not sufficient surplus to spend on new equipment and the business will then need to review the cost of repairing old equipment. A cash flow forecast can be used to investigate the impact of any changes, such as a rise or fall in sales or purchase of supplies, or changes in interest rates on loans or taxes.

A bank may require a copy of the cash flow forecast before they will agree to a loan.

Cash flow vs. balance sheet

Studied

A cash flow forecast shows how money is moving in and out of the business while the balance sheet is a summary of its financial position.

A business will use the cash flow forecast on a month-by-month basis.

Therefore, you could say a cash flow forecast is more useful than a balance sheet. Some people think a balance sheet does not help in planning for the future.

Identify **two** facts and **one** opinion from the following table.

	Fact	Opinion
A cash flow forecast shows how money is moving in and out of the business.		
A balance sheet is a summary of the financial position.		
Therefore, you could say a cash flow forecast is more useful than a balance sheet.		
A business will use the cash flow forecast on a month by month basis.		
Some people think a balance sheet does not help in planning.		

Producing a cash flow forecast

Studied ☐

The information given has been used to produce a cash flow forecast for January to June:

- capital from owner: £10,000
- sales: January £3,000, February £2,500, March to June £2,000 each month
- materials: January £4,000, February £1,000, March to June £500 each month
- rent: £1,000 each month
- council tax: £150 each month
- wages: £300 each month
- equipment: January £2,000
- utility bills: January £500, February to June £150 each month
- insurance: January £400
- advertising: January, April and June £100 each
- telephone: January £100, February to June £40 each month
- repairs: April £300.

CASH FLOW FORECAST							
	January	February	March	April	May	June	TOTAL
Income							
Finance from owner	£10,000						£10,000
Sales		£3,000	£2,500	£2,000	£2,000	£2,000	£11,500
Total income (a)	**£10,000**	**£3,000**	**£2,500**	**£2,000**	**£2,000**	**£2,000**	**£21,500**
Expenditure							
Materials	£4,000	£1,000	£500	£500	£500	£500	£7,000
Rent	£1,000	£1,000	£1,000	£1,000	£1,000	£1,000	£6,000
Council tax	£150	£150	£150	£150	£150	£150	£900
Wages	£300	£300	£300	£300	£300	£300	£1,800
Equipment	£2,000	£0	£0	£0	£0	£0	£2,000
Utility bills/ connection	£500	£150	£150	£150	£150	£150	£1,250
Insurance	£400	£0	£0	£0	£0	£0	£400
Advertising	£100	£0	£0	£100	£0	£100	£300
Telephone	£100	£40	£40	£40	£40	£40	£300
Repairs/renewals	£0	£0	£0	£300	£0	£0	£300
Total expenditure (b)	**£8,550**	**£2,640**	**£2,140**	**£2,540**	**£2,140**	**£2,240**	**£20,250**
Net inflow (a–b)	£1,450	£360	£360	(£540)	(£140)	(£240)	£1,250
Opening balance	£0	£1,450	£1,810	£2,170	£1,630	£1,490	
Closing balance	£1,450	£1,810	£2,170	£1,630	£1,490	£1,250	£1,250

The business can use the cash flow forecast to identify any possible issues with cash flow or any problems from cash surplus or deficit.

In the example cash flow forecast given above, the owner has put £10,000 into the business and six months later the closing balance is a surplus but it is only £1,250. February and March are the only months where the income from sales has been more than the outgoings. In April to June the business is spending more than it has coming in.

The business has only £1,250 in the bank and, if it continues to make only £2000 in income each month and outgoings stay the same, the business will soon not have enough money to cover its outgoings and will be in debt.

The income from sales was high in February, then fell in March and again in April. In April the business has allocated £300 for repairs but this may not be needed because the equipment was only purchased in January.

Learning aim C
Understand how businesses measure success and identify areas for improvement

Learning aim C is an introduction to profit and loss, and financial statements such as the profit and loss account and the balance sheet. It also provides the opportunity to analyse financial statements and to look at how a business can increase its profit margin.

Understand how businesses measure success

This topic focuses on how a business can calculate profit. To plan for the future the business will need to know the cost of sales and how to calculate gross profit.

Making a profit

Cost of sales

The cost of sales is the money used to make the product and will include the materials, wages for employees who produce the product and any other costs for producing the product.

Gross profit

Gross profit is the difference between the costs of making the product – the cost of sales – and the money customers pay – revenue. To calculate gross profit the following formula is used:

gross profit = revenue – cost of sales

For example, if revenue from sales was £3,000 but it cost a business £2,100 to make the product, the gross profit would be:

£900 (gross profit) = £3,000 (revenue) – £2,100 (cost of sales)

The business needs to spend money to buy the materials and labour to make the product and will need to make sufficient money from the sale of the product to cover these costs. If the business sells the products and makes enough money to cover the cost of sales and there is money left over, the business will have a positive gross profit. If the gross profit remains positive for some time, the business will have money for investment in new equipment or expansion.

If the business is selling the products and the revenue does not cover the cost of sales, the business will have a negative gross profit and will be losing money. If the business is not making sufficient money to cover the cost of the materials and labour, the business will have to use any savings or get a loan to cover the costs of sales. If the business continues to have a negative gross profit it will eventually have no money, have debts and will have to close.

Net profit

The net profit is calculated by subtracting all the business's expenses from the gross profit. The formula for calculating net profit is:

net profit = gross profit − expenditure

For example, if the gross profit was £5,000 and the business expenditure was £3,200:

£1,800 (net profit) = £5,000 (gross profit) − £3,200 (expenditure)

If the business has a positive net profit the business is making sufficient money to cover all the business expenses and it is managing its money well. A positive net profit will mean that the business has money left to invest in development or to buy new equipment.

If the business has a negative net profit it is not making enough money – revenue – from selling the products to cover all the costs of making and selling the products. The business will need to investigate why it has a negative net profit. The business may need to look at raising the price of its products to cover its business costs or look at reducing the business costs. Occasionally a fall in sales may be outside the control of the business, such as in a recession when customers may cut back on what they spend.

If a business has a positive gross profit but a negative net profit, it will need to investigate ways of reducing its business expenditure.

Measuring success by looking at financial statements

Studied

Financial statements record the transactions of the business and, at the end of a business's financial year, it has to produce two main documents:

● a profit and loss account (or income statement)
● a balance sheet (or statement of financial position).

Income statement (profit and loss account)

Studied

The profit and loss account is a summary of the business transactions over the financial period, which is usually a one-year period. The profit and loss account will record the business's total income and expenditure and, by deducting the total expenditure from the total income, will identify if the business has made a profit or a loss.

The profit and loss account is produced to show the owners or shareholders how the business is performing, but not all businesses are required by law to produce a profit and loss account. A sole trader or a partnership that is not a limited company does not need to produce a profit and loss account but will need to keep records of their income and expenditure. Limited companies must produce a profit and loss account.

The following information has been used to produce a profit and loss account:

- income from sales: £20,000
- cost of sales: £15,000.

The **gross profit** is the income from sales minus the cost of sales.

Income from sales		£20,000
Cost of sales	£15,000	
Gross profit		£5,000

The next step is to add the expenses/overheads, such as:

- mortgage payment: £1,000
- salaries and wages: £2,000
- electricity: £300
- telephone and internet: £200.

Income from sales		£20,000
Cost of sales	£15,000	
GROSS PROFIT		£5,000
Expenses		
Mortgage payment	£1,000	
Salaries and wages	£2,000	
Electricity	£300	
Telephone and internet	£200	

The final step is to calculate the **net profit**: gross profit minus expenses.

Income from sales		£20,000
Cost of sales	£15,000	
GROSS PROFIT		£5,000
Expenses		
Mortgage payment	£1,000	
Salaries and wages	£2,000	
Electricity	£300	
Telephone and internet	£200	
NET PROFIT		£1,500

You will be provided with figures and will need to produce a profit and loss account. The profit and loss account will incorporate a trading account that records the revenue, the cost of sales and the gross profit.

Statement of financial position (balance sheet)

Studied ■

The **balance sheet** records the business's assets and liabilities; it is called a balance sheet because the total value of the assets is always the same as the total value for the liabilities.

The balance sheet is said to be **a snapshot of the business's financial position**. The balance sheet will record the assets and liabilities of the business at a point in time, but the assets and liabilities will change quickly as the business continues to sell products or purchase from suppliers.

The balance sheet records all the assets and liabilities of the business and the money used to set up the business. The assets are anything owned by the business, such as equipment, stock and furniture, while the liabilities are any debts the business may have.

The balance sheet will record:

- **fixed assets** – items the business needs and will probably keep for some time, such as buildings, fixtures and fittings
- **current assets** – items that can be quickly turned into money, such as stock or money owed by customers
- **current liabilities** – money owed by the business that must be paid back within a year, such as suppliers, short-term loans and overdrafts
- **long-term liabilities** – money owed for more than a year, such as a mortgage or large bank loan

- **capital** – how the business activities are funded; the money can come from either internal sources (invested in the business by the owner, share capital from shareholders, any profits) or external sources (for example, bank loans)
- **net assets** – the balance sheet will show how the business is using the money invested by the owners.

The business will use the balance sheet to review it **working capital**, which is the current assets minus the current liabilities. The business will hope to be in a position where there are more assets than liabilities, but will at least want the current assets to equal the current liabilities. If the current liabilities are more than the current assets the business may not have sufficient money to fund their day-to-day activities such as paying suppliers, wages or utility bills.

You will be provided with figures and will need to produce a balance sheet. For example:

- Building: £2,500
- Fixtures: £200
- Stock: £700
- Debtors: £750
- Bank: £600
- Trade creditors: £500
- Overdraft: £50
- Long-term debt: £200
- Owner capital: £2500
- Profit: £1500.

The following is a step-by-step guide on how to construct a balance sheet from the information provided:

1. The first line will be the business name and the date the balance sheet was produced.
2. This is followed by listing the fixed and current assets and then the current liabilities.
3. The next step is to calculate the net current assets by taking the current liabilities from the current assets.
4. Add the total fixed assets to the net current assets.
5. Record the long-term liabilities.
6. Take the long-term liabilities from the net current assets.
7. Record the capital.

Step 1 BALANCE SHEET FOR CC JEWELLERY AS AT 31 DECEMBER 2012			
Step 2			
ASSETS			
Fixed assets:			
Building	£2,500		
Fixtures	£200		
Total fixed assets		**£2,700**	
Current assets:			
Stock	£700		
Debtors	£750		
Bank	£600		
Total current assets	**£2,050**		
TOTAL ASSETS			**£4,750**
LIABILITIES			
Current liabilities:			
Trade creditors	£500		
Overdraft	£50		
Total current liabilities	**£550**		
Step 3			
Net current assets		£1,500	
Step 4			
Total assets less current liabilities		£4,200	
Step 5			
Long-term liabilities	**£200**		

(Continued)

Step 6			
Net assets		£4,000	
Step 7			
Capital			
Owner capital	£2,500		
Profit	£1,500	**£4,000**	
TOTAL LIABILITIES			**£4,750**

Understand how businesses can be more successful

This topic provides the opportunity to understand how a business can use the information from their financial statements to improve their profits.

A business can use the data in the profit and loss account and the balance sheet to investigate how it could improve and plan for the future. The business will want to increase its profit and could look at reducing costs, producing more products or increasing the selling price of their product or service. If the business is making a profit, they could increase this profit by expanding or looking at developing a new product range.

A business could look at reducing costs to make more profit and this could be achieved by looking for cheaper suppliers or introducing ways to reduce expenditure on bills such as telephone, gas and electricity.

If you look at the balance sheet for CC jewellery the total current assets are £2,050 and the business has only £550 in current liabilities. There are more than sufficient current assets to cover the current liabilities, which means that the business should look at ways to use the money in the bank to improve the business.

If CC jewellery did not sell its stock and the customers were late in paying their accounts, the business still has sufficient money in the bank to pay the trade creditors and its overdraft.

The balance sheet identifies that CC jewellery has very little debt, both short term and long term, and there is sufficient money in the bank and money due from customers to cover all liabilities.

Figure 2.3 CC Jewellery holds a stock of these charm bracelets

Unit 2 External assessment: sample exam 1

1 CC jewellery sells charms and bracelets at local craft fairs.

Which of the following is a start-up cost for CC jewellery? (1)

Tick one of the boxes.

Heating ☐

Income ☐

Raw materials ☐

Staff wages ☐

2 CC jewellery has expanded its business and is using a factory to manufacture the charms.

Give two examples of the fixed costs. (2)

Write your answers in the boxes.

Example 1:

Example 2:

Give two examples of the variable costs. (2)

Example 1:

Example 2:

3 Below is some data about costs at CC Jewellery.

What are the variable costs? **(1)**

Write your answer in the empty cell of the table.

	£
Total costs	2,100
Fixed costs	1,200
Variable costs	

If the variable cost per item was £20, how many items has CC jewellery made? **(1)**

Write your answer in the box.

4 Revenue is money created by the business.

Which two from the following list are revenue? **(2)**

Tick two of the boxes.

Sales income ☐

Expenditure ☐

Overheads ☐

Owner's capital ☐

5 Complete the following:

Revenue = is number of sales ×... **(1)**

If a business sells 80 lipsticks for £1.50 each, what is their revenue? **(1)**

6 CC jewellery sells the bracelets for £2 each. Each bracelet costs CC jewellery £0.50 in raw materials to produce. Total fixed costs are £1,200.

CC jewellery makes and sells 400 bracelets.

What is the sales income? **(1)**

What are the total costs? **(1)**

Does the amount of money created by CC jewellery cover its costs? **(1)**

7 CC jewellery has started trading and needs to know about breakeven.

Explain the term breakeven. (3)

8 CC jewellery has asked for a breakeven analysis, from the information below, to see how they are doing.

- Price: £2.75
- Variable cost: £0.75
- Fixed cost: £1,200

Figure 2.4 CC Jewellery costs and revenue

How many units does CC jewellery need to sell to break even? (1)

Explain how you have reached your decision? (2)

9 The state of the economy has changed and CC jewellery has to pay more for raw materials. There is an increase in their fixed costs and they have increased the selling price.

- Price: £3.29
- Variable cost: £0.89
- Fixed cost: £1,500

Construct a graph to show the breakeven point. **(1)**

Use the formula to check the graph is correct. **(1)**

If CC jewellery can produce 1,200 bracelets, what is the margin of safety? **(1)**

10 A budget will be helpful for CC jewellery.

Which of the following are benefits of having a budget? (1)

Tick the correct boxes.

Plan ahead ☐

Get a loan ☐

Find a new market ☐

Find the best supplier ☐

Make a profit ☐

11

Give two reasons why a budget is a useful tool. (2)

12 Use the information in the table to answer the following questions.

CC jewellery cash flow forecast							
	Jan	**Feb**	**Mar**	**Apr**	**May**	**Jun**	**Jul**
Cash in bank	50,000	-54,000	-43,000	-38,000	-27,000	-16,000	-11,000
Receipts							
Cash in sales	0	15,000	15,000	15,000	15,000	15,000	15,000
Total cash	50,000	-39,000	-28,000	-23,000	-12,000	-1,000	4,000
Payments							
Premises	60,000						
Equipment	40,000						
Wages	2,000	2,000	2,000	2,000	2,000	2,000	2,000
Telephone	800	800	800	800	800	800	800
Maintenance	1,200	1,200	1,200	1,200	1,200	1,200	1,200
Heating & Lighting			6,000			6,000	
Total Payments	104,000	4,000	10,000	4,000	4,000	10,000	4,000
Opening bank balance	50,000	-54,000	-43,000	-38,000	-27,000	-16,000	-11,000
Closing bank balance	-54,000	-43,000	-38,000	-27,000	-16,000	-11,000	0

Identify *one* inflow of money. (1)

Identify *one* outflow of money. (1)

How much cash does CC jewellery have at the start of August? (1)

Why is there such a large negative closing balance in January? (2)

13 Some numbers are missing from CC jewellery's profit and loss account.

	2011 (£)
Revenue	8,000
Cost of sales	5,000
GROSS PROFIT	
Rent	400
Wages	1,000
Heating and lighting	100
Telephone	60
Interest	40
NET PROFIT	

What should the figure for gross profit be? (1)

What should the figure for net profit be? (1)

14 Look at these figures from CC jewellery's profit and loss accounts.

	2010 (£)	2011 (£)
Revenue	8,000	10,000
Cost of sales	4,000	6,000
GROSS PROFIT	4,000	4,000
Rent	400	800
Salaries and wages	1,000	1,000
Heating and lighting	60	60
Utilities	50	60
Interest	50	40
NET PROFIT	2,440	2,040

Comment on CC jewellery's gross and net profit, and explain why there was a smaller net profit in 2011 than 2010. (4)

15 Complete the following statement:

A balance sheet is a summary of… (1)

Tick one of the boxes.

…money flowing into and out of the business ☐

…sales and expenses ☐

…assets and liabilities ☐

…the business's marketing campaign ☐

16

Give three examples of current assets. (3)

Example 1:

Example 2:

Example 3:

17

What is the formula for calculating net current assets? (1)

Tick one of the boxes.

Fixed assets – current assets ☐

Fixed assets – current liabilities ☐

Current liabilities – current assets ☐

Current assets – current liabilities ☐

18 Look at the information in the balance sheet below.

BALANCE SHEET FOR CC JEWELLERY AS AT 31 DECEMBER 2010		
ASSETS		
Fixed assets		
Buildings and fixtures	£2,700	
Total fixed assets		£2,700
Current assets		
Stock	£700	
Debtors	£750	
Bank	£850	
Total current assets	£2,300	
TOTAL ASSETS		?
LIABILITIES		
Current liabilities		
Trade creditors	£750	
Overdraft	£50	
Total current liabilities	**?**	
Net current assets		?

Calculate the value of the total assets for CC jewellery. **(1)**

Calculate the total current liabilities. **(1)**

Calculate the net current assets for CC jewellery. **(1)**

19 Look at the information in the following balance sheet.

BALANCE SHEET FOR GOWN LTD AS AT 31 DECEMBER 2011		
ASSETS		
Fixed assets		
Buildings and fixtures	£3,500	
Total fixed assets		£3,500
Current assets		
Stock	£200	
Debtors	£800	
Bank	£150	
Total current assets	£1,150	
TOTAL ASSETS		£4,650
LIABILITIES		
Current liabilities		
Trade creditors	£600	
Overdraft	£300	
Total current liabilities	£900	
Net current assets		£250

Evaluate the performance of Gown Ltd. (5)

Unit 2 External assessment: sample exam 2

1

Give two examples of direct costs. (2)

Example 1:

Example 2:

2

Explain what running costs are. (2)

3 CC jewellery sells charms and bracelets at local craft fairs.

The total costs for CC jewellery will be... **(1)**

Tick the correct box to complete the statement.

Fixed costs plus the price of the charms ☐

Fixed costs plus variable costs ☐

Fixed costs minus variable costs ☐

Variable costs plus the price of the charms ☐

4 A bracelet costs £0.50 in raw materials to produce and the total fixed costs are now £1,200.

How much does it cost to make 400 bracelets? **(1)**

£1,400 ☐

£1,200.50 ☐

£2,000 ☐

£1,600 ☐

5

Explain what revenue is and how it is calculated. (2)

6 CC jewellery sells the charms for £2.50 each. Each charm costs CC jewellery £1.50 in raw materials to produce. Total fixed costs are £1,000. CC jewellery makes and sells 500 charms.

What is the sales income? (1)

What is the total cost? (1)

Does the amount of money generated by sales cover the costs? Show how you have reached your decision. (2)

7 CC jewellery has started trading and needs to know about breakeven.

What is the formula for calculating breakeven? **(1)**

8 Look at the following graph.

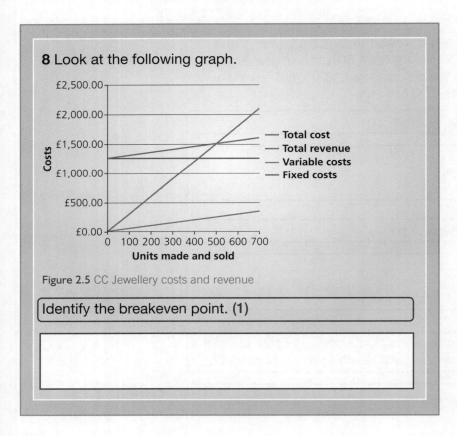

Figure 2.5 CC Jewellery costs and revenue

Identify the breakeven point. **(1)**

9 Look at the following information from CC jewellery.

- Price: £2.75
- Variable cost: £0.75
- Fixed cost: £1,200

Calculate the breakeven point. Remember to show your workings. **(1)**

10

Explain the term 'budgetary control'. **(3)**

11

Give three reasons why budgeting is important. **(3)**

Reason 1:

Reason 2:

Reason 3:

12 Look at the following cash flow forecast for CC jewellery.

CC jewellery Cash Flow Forecast						
	Apr	**May**	**Jun**	**Jul**	**Aug**	**Sep**
Cash in bank	-3,000	-7,000	-1,000	-1,000	-5,000	1,000
Receipts						
Cash in sales	15,000	15,000	15,000	15,000	15,000	15,000
Total cash	12,000	8,000	14,000	14,000	10,000	16,000
Payments						
Premises	5,000	5,000	5,000	5,000	5,000	5,000
Equipment	10,000			10,000		
Wages	2,000	2,000	2,000	2,000	2,000	2,000
Telephone	800	800	800	800	800	800
Maintenance	1,200	1,200	1,200	1,200	1,200	1,200
Heating & Lighting			6,000			6,000
Total Payments	19,000	9,000	15,000	19,000	9,000	15,000
Opening bank balance	-3,000	-7,000	-1,000	-1,000	-5,000	1,000
Closing bank balance	-7,000	-1,000	-1,000	-5,000	1,000	1,000

Identify why there was a problem with CC jewellery's cash flow in July. (1)

In which month did it show its first surplus? (1)

Explain two ways that CC Jewellery could improve its cash flow. (4)

13. Look at the figures given below.

	2011 (£)
Revenue	11,500
Cost of sales	4,000
GROSS PROFIT	?
Mortgage	3,500
Wages	1,000
Insurance	2,000
Admin	450
Interest on loan	400
NET PROFIT	?

What is the gross profit for 2011? Show your workings. (1)

What is the net profit for 2011? Show your workings. (1)

14 Here are the profit and loss figures for two years of trading at CC Jewellery.

Fill in the missing figures. (4)

CC jewellery profit and loss accounts		
	2010	**2011**
Sales	£2,645	£2,833
Cost of sales		£1,464
Gross profit	£1,447	
Expenses		£1,204
Net profit	£535	

Explain what happened to the profits in 2011. (2)

15 This is the profit and loss account for FF Glow in 2011.

FF Glow profit and loss account	
	2011
Sales	£3,590
Cost of sales	£1,300
Gross profit	**£2,290**
Expenses	
Rent	£600
Heating	£400
Advertising	£250
Wages	£700
Admin	£200
Total expenses	£2,150
Net profit	**£140**

Using these figures, **outline** what the business could do to improve the situation. (4)

16

What is meant by the term 'current liability'? (1)

Give an example of a current liability. (1)

17

What is meant by the term 'current asset'? (1)

Give an example of a current asset. (1)

18 Use the information in this balance sheet to complete the following calculations.

BALANCE SHEET FOR LH HANDCREAMS AS AT 31 DECEMBER 2011		
ASSETS		
Fixed assets		
Buildings and fixtures	£2,700	
Total fixed assets		£2,700
Current assets		
Stock	**?**	
Debtors	£900	
Bank	£550	
Total current assets	£1,600	
TOTAL ASSETS		**?**
LIABILITIES		
Current liabilities		
Trade creditors	£1,400	
Overdraft	£300	
Total current liabilities	£1,700	
Net current assets		**?**

What are the total assets? (1)

What is the figure for stock? (1)

What are the net current assets? (1)

19 Look at this extract taken from a balance sheet.

BALANCE SHEET FOR GOWNS LTD AS AT 31 DECEMBER 2011		
ASSETS		
Fixed assets		
Equipment	£3,000	
Total fixed assets		£3,000
Current assets		
Stock	£500	
Debtors	£800	
Bank	£200	
Total current assets	£1,500	
TOTAL ASSETS		£4,500
LIABILITIES		
Current liabilities		
Trade creditors	£1,100	
Loan	£400	
Total current liabilities	£1,500	
Net current assets		£0

Suggest **two** actions that Gowns Ltd could take to improve their current trading position. (4)

Answers: Unit 1 Knowledge recap questions

Learning aim A Know how trends and the current business environment may impact on a business

1. Websites, newspapers, questionnaires.
2. It may be out of date or it may be biased – it could be someone's personal opinion.
3. **a.** Inflation, exchange rates, taxation.
   b. Unemployment levels, location of suppliers, access to suitable staff.
4.

Social	Ethical	Technological	Environmental
Flexitime Working from home	Testing on animals Carbon footprint	Online shopping Mobile barcode scanning	Use of solar panels Recyclable materials

5. **a.** Fewer than nine people.
   b. 10–49 people.
   c. 50–249 people.
   d. 250+ people
6. The chances are that the business is up and running and successful. This means somebody else took the risks, made the mistakes and got it working properly. It should be better placed to get financial help as it has a track record. It may have lots of suppliers, whereas a start-up business may only have one. It should have an existing customer base, so you'll get a wage/salary/share of the profits straightaway. In a sense the risk is less.
7. It will almost certainly be more expensive than starting from a small base, so more actual money might be at risk. It is still somebody else's idea and not yours, so it may not be quite the way you'd have done it if you had built it up yourself. There may be other stakeholders who have a say in how it is run and that might not suit what you want.

Learning aim B Plan an idea for a new business

1. Is there a gap in the market? Can I produce/ service it on an on-going basis? How will I get the product or service to the customers? Have I got sufficient money to start up and keep it running properly till it gets established? How much competition is there and how will it react?
2. A business would know it was successful by reviewing sales figures and profits. A business could use feedback from customer surveys or feedback from any communications with customers to identify if the customers were satisfied with its products.
3. A – benefits then work on the features.
4. The business would need to ensure that it met the needs of existing customers by carrying out market research to find out what the customers' wants and needs are. The business would need to review and, when necessary, amend its products to meets the needs of its customers. The business will also need to monitor the products and services offered by its competitors.

Learning aim C Present a business model for a business start-up

1. Both sell shares but a limited company can only sell its shares privately. A PLC can sell its shares to the general public.
2.

Sole trader	Limited company	Franchise
Unlimited liability Take holidays when you want	Limited liability Has a board of directors	Company provides all the training for you Only sell what the company says you can

3. You only lose up to the amount you invest, so if you invest £10,000 and the business goes bust and owes £250,000, you only lose your £10,000. You are not liable for the rest of the debt.
4.

They set the aims and objectives of the business, then the strategy to achieve these	Directors
They run the business on a day-to-day basis	Managers
They invest in the business in the hope of making a profit	Shareholders

Answers

115

5. **Aims** are long-term goals, often a vision of where you want the business to be.
Example 1: I want the business to be profitable after two years of trading.
Example 2: I want the business to contribute to the local community.
Objectives support aims (not the other way round) by giving specific targets and strategies that can be measured to meet the aims.
Example 1: From the aim above I would set six-monthly targets of sales, costs and revenue to see if they matched what I thought would happen. If they didn't I would change what I was doing to get back on course and revise the plan.
Example 2: From the aim above I would employ local people to help with the business rather than go elsewhere. If the business was going well and I needed to expand, I would consult with the local community about any possible adverse effects, such as pollution.

6. The local community has several interests. It will be keen to ensure there is no adverse pollution caused by smell, extra transport and unsightly buildings that may cause properties to devalue. On the other hand, the new business may provide employment for some of the villagers, which would be a good thing.
The bank will need to know if its investment is going to be repaid, not just immediately but on an on-going basis. It will need to know that there is a sufficient market for the business to be sustainable over time, which will make the investment safe. If the business looks good, the bank will not want to miss out on being part of a successful venture.

Answers: Unit 2 External assessment

Sample exam 1

1. Raw materials.

Assessor comment: Heating and staff wages are not start-up costs, and income is not a cost.

2. **a.** Fixed costs – rent, insurance.
   b. Variable costs – raw materials, staff wages.
3. **a.** Variable costs are £900
      (£2,100 – £1,200 = £900).
   b. 45 (£900/20 = 45).
4. Sales income and Owner's capital.

Assessor comment: Expenditure and overheads are costs.

5. **a.** Revenue = sales × price per item
   b. Revenue = 80 × £1.50 = £120.
9.

6. **a.** Sales income = 400 × £2 = £800
   b. Total costs = £1,200 + £200 = £1,400
   c. The business is not covering its costs because the sales income is £800 and the costs are £1,400.
7. Breakeven is when the money from sales is the same as the cost of producing the product (1 mark), and the business makes no profit and no loss (1 mark). The business can use breakeven to find out how many products they will need to sell to cover their costs (1 mark).
8. **a.** CC jewellery will need to make 600 to break even.
   b. This is where total revenue and total costs cross on the graph; it's where CC jewellery will not make a profit or a loss.

Figure 3.1

a. The graph shows that about 625 units need to be sold.
b. The formula is 1,500/(3.29 – 0.89) = 625; this confirms the information on the graph.
c. The margin of safety is 1,200 – 625 = 575; CC jewellery can still produce more and make more profit.

10. Plan ahead.

Assessor comment: The purpose of a budget is to set targets for income and expenditure, i.e. to plan ahead.

11. Budgeting will help identify the money expected from sales and what the business will need to pay out (1 mark). It will help identify where cuts can be made in spending (1 mark).

Assessor comment: It would also be correct to say that budgeting will help a business decide if it can continue to trade as it is or that to continue trading the business must make cuts in its spending or look for ways to increase sales.

12. a. An inflow is cash sales.
b. An outflow is money spent on equipment.
c. There is £0 in the bank at the start of August.
d. No money from sales (1 mark), large expenditures on premises and equipment (1 mark).
13. a. Gross profit = £3,000
b. Net profit = £1,400.
14. CC jewellery has made both positive gross and net profits in each year (2 marks). Revenue has increased in the second year but gross profit is the same for each year (1 mark). Net profit has gone down in 2011 because rent has doubled while other expenses remained the same (1 mark).
15. …assets and liabilities.

Assessor comment: The balance sheet is *only* a summary of assets and liabilities at any given moment.

16. Three current assets are: money owed by customers, stock, and money in the bank.
17. Current assets – current liabilities.
18. a. Total assets = £5,000 (£2,700 + £2,300 = £5,000)

Assessor comment: The answer is calculated by adding the total of the fixed assets to the total of the current assets.

b. Total current liabilities = £800 (£750 + £50 = £800)

Assessor comment: The answer is calculated by adding the trade creditors to the overdraft.

c. Net current assets = £1,500 (£2,300 – £800 = £1,500)

Assessor comment: The answer is calculated by taking the total current liabilities away from the total current assets.

19. Gown Ltd has more in current assets (£1,150) than in current liabilities (£900), which is a good position to be in (1 mark). Gown Ltd would have enough to pay its overdraft and debtors (1 mark). There is not enough money in the bank to pay the overdraft (1 mark). Most of the current assets are money owed by customers (1 mark). If Gown does not get the money from the customers it will not be able to pay its creditors (1 mark).

Sample exam 2

1. Raw materials, labour.
2. Running costs are those costs a business has to pay out on a day-to-day basis (1 mark) so that it can continue to trade by paying staff and suppliers, and have something to sell (1 mark). They must be paid to keep suppliers, staff and customers happy.
3. Fixed costs plus variable costs.

Assessor comment: 'Fixed costs plus the price of the charms' and 'variable costs plus the price of the charms' are wrong as price is not a cost: 'Fixed costs minus variable costs' is wrong because it is plus and not minus.

4. £1,400 (400 × £0.50 = £200, then add this to £1,200 to get £1,400).

Assessor comment: It is always beneficial to show the working out because, if the final answer is incorrect, marks may be awarded for using the correct formula.

5. Revenue is the money a business gets from selling its products or services to customers (1 mark). Revenue is calculated by sales price multiplied by the number of items sold (1 mark).
6. a. Sales income = 500 × £2.50 = £1,250
b. Total cost = £1,000 + (£1.50 × 500) = £1,750
c. The business is not covering its costs because the sales income is £1,250 and the costs are £1,750. The business is only getting £1,250 from sales and needs to pay out £1,750. It needs £500 more to cover its bills.
7. breakeven =

$$\frac{\text{fixed costs}}{\text{selling price per item} - \text{variable cost per item}}$$

8. The cross should be placed where the lines cross above 500 units.

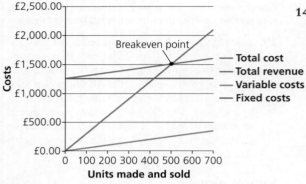

Figure 3.2

9. Breakeven = fixed cost/(price – variable cost)
Breakeven = £1,200/(£2.75 – £0.75)
Breakeven = £1,200/£2.00 = £600.

10. Budgetary control is where a business prepares its budget and then reviews it to see how it has performed against its planned figures (1 mark). Budgetary control will identify whether the business is achieving its targets (1 mark) and where it needs to make changes to reduce expenditure so that it can increase or maintain profits (1 mark).

11. Reason 1: A budget will identify where the business plans to get its income from and how it will spend it.
Reason 2: Budgets will help identify if there is money to buy equipment or expand.
Reason 3: Budgets will identify where and how the business is spending its income and if there are areas where spending could be reduced.

12.a. The business expenditure was £19,000 but it only had £15,000 from sales.
b. August was the first month the business makes a profit.
c. CC jewellery could look for a cheaper supplier for its heating and lighting, or look at ways to reduce its bills (2 marks). The business could look at the amount it is paying in maintenance and whether there is really a need for all the planned purchase of equipment (2 marks).

13.a. Gross profit = £11,500 – £4,000 = £7,500
b. Net profit = £7,500 – (£3,500 + £1,000 + £2,000 + £450 + £400) = £150

14.

CC jewellery profit and loss accounts		
	2010	**2011**
Sales	£2,645	£2,833
Cost of sales	**£1,198**	£1,464
Gross profit	£1,447	**£1,369**
Expenses	**£912**	£1,204
Net profit	£535	**£165**

The gross profit in 2011 is less than the gross profit in 2010 (1 mark) while the net profit is less in 2011 because there is a big increase in the expenses (1 mark).

15. The business could look at ways to reduce the cost of sales, which will give it a bigger gross profit (1 mark). The business could look at ways to reduce its administration (1 mark) and advertising (1 mark) bills, which would mean more net profits. The business could look at ways to reduce its heating bill, for example by switching to a cheaper supplier (1 mark).

16.a. A current liability is something the business owes and must pay back in the short term.
b. One example of a current liability is an overdraft.

17.a. A current asset is something the business has that it can turn into money.
b. An example of a current asset is money in the bank.

18.a. Total assets = £2,700 + £1,600 = £4,300
b. Stock = £1,600 – £900 – £550 = £150
c. Net current assets = £1,600 – £1,700 = -£100

19. Gowns Ltd owes a lot of money to its creditors and must look at ways to pay its suppliers or it will not be able to get any more credit (2 marks). Gowns Ltd should get its customers to pay their bills quicker or on time so that it can pay the creditors (2 marks).

Index

Index